THE CHALLENGE OF OUR CULTURE

The
CHALLENGE
of Our
CULTURE

CLARENCE TUCKER CRAIG
Editor

Essay Index Reprint Series

BOOKS FOR LIBRARIES PRESS
FREEPORT, NEW YORK

Originally published as Volume One of
The Interseminary Series.

Copyright 1946 by Harper & Brothers.

Reprinted 1972 by arrangement with
Harper & Row, Publishers, Inc.

Library of Congress Cataloging in Publication Data

Craig, Clarence Tucker, 1895-1953, ed.
  The challenge of our culture.

  (The Interseminary series, v. 1) (Essay index
reprint series)
  Includes bibliographies.
  1. Culture--Addresses, essays, lectures.
2. Christianity--20th century--Addresses, essays,
lectures. 3. Church and social problems--Addresses,
essays, lectures. I. Title. II. Series.
[BR115.C8C69]   261.8   70-167331
ISBN 0-8369-2765-6

PRINTED IN THE UNITED STATES OF AMERICA
BY
NEW WORLD BOOK MANUFACTURING CO., INC.
HALLANDALE, FLORIDA 33009

CONTENTS

PREFACE

THE INTERSEMINARY SERIES

The five volumes which comprise "The Interseminary Series"
have three main purposes: to outline the character of the
contemporary world which challenges the Church; to pro-
claim afresh the nature of the gospel and the Church which
must meet that challenge; and to set forth the claims which
ecumenical Christianity makes upon the various churches as
they face their world task. Although the perspective of the
volumes is American, it is nevertheless comprehensive in that
it views the Church as the Body of Christ in the world, per-
forming a mission to the whole world.

The immediate occasion for the publication of the series is
a national conference of theological students scheduled for
June, 1947 under the auspices and initiative of the Interseminary Movement in the United States. The volumes will
serve as study material for the delegates to the conference.

From the outset, however, it has been the desire and aim of
those sponsoring the project that the volumes might have a
wide appeal. They have been designed for the Christian public
in general, in the hope that there may be in them help toward
our common Christian task in the fateful postwar days.

To produce the volumes, the Interseminary Committee outlined the five major questions and organized the Commissions
which are listed below. Each Commission met once, and in the

course of a two-day meeting outlined, first, the chapters for its respective volume, and, second, the main elements to be contained in each chapter. Authors were assigned from within the Commission. A first draft of each paper was submitted to Commission members and the chairman of the Commission for criticism, returned and subsequently rewritten in final form. The fifth volume, which is a summary interpretation of the preceding statements, is written by a single author. It should be specially noted that the work of Commission I-B was graciously undertaken by the already organized Pacific Coast Theological Group to which were added a few guests for the purpose at hand.

The volumes thus represent a combination of group thinking and individual effort. They are not designed to be completely representative statements to which the Commissions, or the Interseminary Movement, would subscribe. They are intended, rather, to convey information and to stimulate thought, in the earnest hope that this may in turn contribute to a more faithful performance of our Christian mission in the world.

For the National Interseminary Committee:
Robert S. Bilheimer
Executive Secretary

THE AUTHORS

ELMER J. F. ARNDT is professor of philosophy of religion at Eden Theological Seminary. Following undergraduate work at Tulane, he has taken the B.D. degree at Eden Seminary, the M.A. from Washington University, the S.T.M. from Union Theological Seminary and the Ph.D. from Yale. He is chairman of the Commission on Social Action of the Evangelical and Reformed Church, and a member of the American Philosophical Association and the American Theological Association. Dr. Arndt is a member of the Evangelical and Reformed Church.

CLARENCE TUCKER CRAIG, until 1946 professor of New Testament language and literature at Oberlin Graduate School of Theology, holds the A.B. degree from Morningside College and the S.T.B. and Ph.D. from Boston University. In addition he has done graduate work at Harvard, Basle and the University of Berlin. Among his publications are *Jesus in Our Teaching; We Have an Altar; The Study of the New Testament; The Beginning of Christianity;* and *One God, One World.* In the autumn of 1946 Dr. Craig assumed new duties as professor of New Testament at Yale Divinity School. Dr. Craig is a member of the Methodist Church.

BUELL G. GALLAGHER is professor of Christian ethics in the Pacific School of Religion, Berkeley, California. He holds the

ix

B.A. degree from Carleton College, the B.D. from Union Theological Seminary, the Ph.D. from Columbia University, and the D.D. from Oberlin College. His publications include *American Caste and the Negro College; Color and Conscience: The Irrepressible Conflict;* and *Portrait of a Pilgrim: A Search for the Christian Way in Race Relations.* Dr. Gallagher is a member of the Congregational-Christian Church.

JOSEPH HAROUTUNIAN, who was born in Turkey, studied at the American University in Beirut and has his A.B. and Ph.D. degrees from Columbia University. His B.D. degree was taken at Union Theological Seminary. At present he is professor of systematic theology at McCormick Theological Seminary. He is the author of *Piety versus Moralism* and *Wisdom and Folly in Religion.* Dr. Haroutunian is a member of the Presbyterian Church U.S.A.

WALTER M. HORTON received the A.B. degree from Harvard, the B.D. and S.T.M. from Union Theological Seminary, and the M.A. and Ph.D. from Columbia. In addition, he has taken graduate work at the Sorbonne, the University of Strasbourg and Marburg. Since 1926 he has been Fairchild professor of theology at Oberlin Graduate School of Theology. His most recent publications include *Contemporary English Theology; God; Contemporary Continental Theology; Can Christianity Save Civilization?;* and *Our Eternal Contemporary.* Dr. Horton is a member of the Congregational-Christian Church.

JAMES H. NICHOLS is assistant professor of Church history at the Divinity School of the University of Chicago, and a member of the Federated Theological Faculty. His A.B. degree and his Ph.D. are from Yale University. Dr. Nichols is a member of the Presbyterian Church U.S.A.

AMOS N. WILDER, whose B.A., B.D. and Ph.D. are all from Yale, is professor of New Testament interpretation in the Chicago Theological Seminary, and in the Federated Theological Faculty of the University of Chicago. His further publications include *Eschatology and Ethics in the Teaching of Jesus; Spiritual Aspects of the New Poetry; The Healing of the Waters* (Poems) ; and "The Christian Tradition in Modern Culture," an article in *The Vitality of the Christian Tradition.* Dr. Wilder is a member of the Congregational-Christian Church.

THE CHALLENGE OF OUR CULTURE

1 INTRODUCTION

THE FAITH BY WHICH WE SEE

Clarence Tucker Craig

A CHRISTIAN minister must know the world in which he lives. Otherwise, the relevance of the Christian message will be lost. No one can effectively mediate the vision of God to a world which is hidden from his own eyes by a veil of illusion. When I was in seminary, a physician addressed us with the vehement accusation, "You preachers talk as if we in the pews were a bunch of saints. We're not." And he proceeded to give a damning description out of his medical experience of a humanity which was vicious and corrupt as well as diseased.

In this volume, six of our contemporary Christian thinkers look out upon the world of our time. It is a disturbing picture which they see and one which should provoke long heart-searching. No one will charge any of the authors with sanctimonious complacency. They are not living in some ivory tower of religious contemplation but amid the troubled realities of the twentieth century. Their portrayal is not drawn as an indictment; they simply seek to hold up the mirror to ourselves. No attempt has been made to draw an accurate balance sheet. Not all of the credit items on the ledger have been listed. The objective is not to present exact scientific evaluations but to make us more keenly aware of the paganism of

1

our time. If the chapters contain more of the stinging vehemence of an Amos than the calm analysis of a professional sociologist, I do not regret it. A ministry without a sense of crusading mission is not worth recruiting. If the authors provoke the reader to thought, they will not be disturbed if disagreement should sometimes arise.

What anyone sees depends upon two things. The first is the world in which he lives; in New York skyscrapers and buses are seen rather than pagodas and rickshaws; it was the reverse in Canton, China, in 1915. The second factor is the point of reference from which the world is viewed. Broadway does not look the same at a height of ten thousand feet as it does in the midst of the milling crowd. These two factors are inescapable in the very nature of human experience. No time need be wasted in refuting a solipsism which believes that the world is only the creation of the mind which beholds it. Of course the mind carries on constitutive activity, but the external world possesses a reality which is independent of the individual observer. We do need, however, to guard against the expectation that anyone can ever have a completely objective view of facts and nothing but facts. A science without presuppositions was the ideal of a naïve period when man forgot that every observation is made from some particular point of view. While the combination of many different observations may correct certain types of distortion, there is no way in which the world may be viewed by mortal eyes from an absolute standpoint. Certain presuppositions may be found useful in attaining certain results; some assumptions are more true than others. But there is no possibility of avoiding an initial act of faith by which the world scene is viewed in a particular perspective.

The inevitability of presuppositions does not mean the tacit acceptance of prejudice. Prejudice refuses to look at some of the facts. It prefers to retain its uncritical assumptions and tries to keep them free from examination by others. Unless we have access to the facts, we live in a world of distorted unreality. That is why the unhampered dissemination of information is so important. Without freedom in the interchange of ideas it is impossible to obtain a true view. Dogmatisms always fear free inquiry; those who hold them are unwilling to allow their assumptions to be examined. A faith that has confidence in itself invites the fullest investigation. A fuller knowledge of the facts is a condition for the reduction of prejudice. But no accumulation of information can alter the situation that the world must be approached in terms of some presupposition.

Scientific investigation starts with the assumption of mechanism. The possibility of the intrusion of some external factor would rule out any attempt at exact calculation. That does not mean that science has proved the existence of a universal mechanism. In fact, any such conclusion would make human experience utterly meaningless. It only means that any given body of phenomena may be studied mechanistically and the conclusions thus reached will work within the range of their applicability. It is futile for religious people to protest against the mechanistic assumptions of science and try to smuggle some other factor into laboratory investigation. But it is also naïve when men of science imagine that they have dealt with *all* of reality rather than simply one aspect.

The presupposition which underlies these essays is of another character. It is upon a different plane and has an entirely different type of validity; yet it does likewise have a molding effect upon what is seen. Our authors look out on the world scene through eyes which are controlled by Christian faith. It would be foolish to deny that fact. They have worn no blinkers to shut from view unpleasant evidence which might tend to undermine their faith. A faith which is afraid of the evidence is too feeble to live in the modern world. A faith which leaves some evidence out of the picture is suspect. Nevertheless, no one need apologize for the fact that he looks at the world from a definite point of view. The only question concerns the adequacy of that vantage point to give meaningful perspective to what we see.

The live alternatives to Christian faith are not numerous. Some of them will be discussed as part of the current scene. Over much of the world the Marxist faith in dialectical materialism is the leading competitor. Important as this is, it cannot compare with naturalistic humanism as the claimant for allegiance in contemporary America. In that faith we find a series of assumptions about the neutrality of the universe, the possibilities of man, and the hope for the future which stand in marked contrast to the Christian point of view. The nature of our Christian faith will be set forth first in a later volume. Here we intend only to glance at a few aspects which profoundly affect what our writers see in the world about them.

Our faith begins and ends with the reality and activity of God. This means that the material world itself is not ultimate; it is the creation of God. This means that mechanism can never be the last word; God comes into personal relations with men. Difficult as it is to conceive what personality means apart from the human limitations with which we ordinarily connect the world, it can never be adequate to refer to the ground of our existence as "It." Only persons are self-conscious, make moral decisions, and choose the purposes which they intend to follow. All these characterize what the Christian means by God, and so he persists unabashed in the use of personal symbols, certain that they alone are appropriate to describe the ground of our existence.

The Ultimate is not neutral material out of which man carves his own best destiny. He is a friendly power. This faith must not be misunderstood in terms of the egocentric selfishness of much of the religion about us. That would judge the friendliness of God on the basis of a preponderance of good over evil fortune. The evidence is not to be sought in the pleasant circumstances which favor a few at some time. According to that type of argument the disasters which just as certainly come to other good people would as truly prove an ultimate unfriendliness. Christian belief rests rather upon the conviction that moral order is at the basis of the universe just as surely as the natural order discoverable through science. Man possesses a certain freedom to flout that order. The conditions portrayed in this volume amply demonstrate that fact. So does the concern of the authors and their devotion to the changing of these conditions. This freedom is part of the friendliness of the universe. We do not belong to an order where puppets are protected from all harm, but where character may grow to spiritual maturity.

Yet this mysterious universe presents us with extremely varied pictures. Amid all this bewildering maze, where is the surest clew to the fundamental purpose of the Author of all existence? Christian faith points to an event which came amid the ongoing Jewish experience of the righteousness and mercy of God. This does not involve the life of one who found ease and good fortune attending his efforts. He is one who climaxed his career of courageous love and perfect trust by undergoing a cruel crucifixion. Out of such apparent defeat came the realization of a redemptive victory of God, for He had raised this Jesus from the dead. Here was the central revelation of forgiving grace and overcoming power. Christ is the clew by which we know the ultimate Determiner of destiny.

Christian faith also makes certain presuppositions about man. They are not the romantic illusions according to which man needs only a little more wisdom and good will to solve all his problems. Christian faith sees man from two points of view. According to one, he is a child of God, destined to eternal fellowship with the Creator of life. According to the other, man is a rebellious creature, a being divided against himself and the universe in which he lives. "Earth might be fair" is a conviction which unites all our contributors despite their dissatisfaction with the current scene. Yet the root of these disorders lies in man himself, who does not achieve the good he wills. Nevertheless, he may never be treated as "the scum of the earth" for his true destiny is to be the "salt of the earth."

In the midst of human perplexity there is a community with Christ as its center, which is the promise and foretaste of a new society. No one of our contributors has any illusions about the institutions which bear the name of churches. As in the picture drawn in the Matthaean parables, these organizations include a mixture of wheat and weeds. They partake of the infirmities of their human membership and the limitations of historical existence. At the same time they partake of that redeemed fellowship which is a new brotherhood in the Spirit. Within its fellowship are those who have experienced the joy of forgiveness and therefore should be controlled in their conduct by love for all men. Here is found the living center of God's rule and the prophecy of a universal rule which must include men of every tribe and nation and kindred and tongue.

The consummation of such a society does not lie amid the contradictions of history. True, this rule impinges on every moment of time both in judgment and in hope; but its full realization waits upon the putting off of mortal limitations. "Becoming" must always be the mark of historical process; hence the kingdom of God is never completely here. The Christian has invincible faith in the victory of God. Yet confidence in the high destiny of man and in the beloved society of the eternal world does not divert his attention from the crises of the temporal scene. It is just because of these potentialities that the Christian believer can never view with calmness the exploitations and injustices of an order which thwarts his true being.

Such is a rough and incomplete sketch of the convictions which color the contemporary scene as it is viewed in the following chapters. Individually the authors would probably have phrased these beliefs in differing terminology. But all join in affirming the fact of God, who in Christ has provided redemption for a sinful mankind, a redemption now experienced in the fellowship of a people of God, and one which anticipates His eternal rule. There has been no attempt at this point to give either a complete or an adequate statement of Christian beliefs. But these paragraphs may serve to set the following chapters in closer relation to the fuller expositions in the later volumes of this series.

As they have looked out through the eyes of their faith, our collaborators have seen a world absorbed in the material things made possible by our multiplication of machines. They have perceived the growing importance of economic rivalries amid the competition for power. They have looked with shame at the system of caste built upon color which presents so flagrant a denial of the democratic and Christian convictions which we profess. They observe conflict rather than peace, disintegration rather than increasing unity. They see widespread bewilderment and crippling fears, people whose lives are an unresolved civil war. Amid the moral and spiritual perplexities, Christians seem as hesitant and confused as the rest of men. It would be easy to sink into the slough of despond at such a discouraging sight, but they never do. For they are sure that hope may lie beyond repentance and judgment.

The theme which seems to unite these varied essays is the depersonalization of our modern life. Responsible personal relationships characterize less and less of our existence. Here lies the fundamental antithesis to the Christian viewpoint. According to our faith, individual persons must find their adjustment to a God who meets them on a personal level of experience. Only personal analogies can adequately express man's relation to Him. But a culture which treats man and makes man less than a person presents a fundamental challenge to Christian' convictions. No matter how magnificent may be the outward appearance of a civilization, when it leads to the depersonalization of individuals, it ends in the destruction rather than the gaining of life. The forces which produce this depersonalization are not "signs" of the kingdom of God but warnings of judgment and spiritual death.

Some of the contributors have explored their theme in the light of history, for the present moment is never understandable except in some wider relationship. Every age is a link between an unalterable yesterday and a tomorrow which at least may be influenced by our courage and our faith. We must not repeat the mistakes of yesterday, disdaining to examine the warnings from the past. On the other hand, the failures of days gone by must not sap our daring or keep us from attempting greater things for God in our own time. If we cannot learn from history those interpreters must be right after all who see a succession of recurring cycles. Youth especially need to guard against belittling the voice of experience while at the same time they steadfastly refuse to be cowed or disheartened by the painful pages in the record of the past.

Diagnosis is never enough for curing the ills of mankind. A catalogue of symptoms will not suffice by itself. But this volume is not intended to stand by itself. Its function is served if a merciless searchlight has been turned upon the world of which we are a part. Its aim has been achieved if in personal humility and repentance, young men and women resolve to have their part under God in mediating healing and redemptive faith. It seeks to sound a trumpet call for ministers of God who will match an hour like this with their intelligent devotion, who will find their "call" in the crisis in which we stand and say with the prophet of old, "Lord, here am I; send me."

2

MEN AMONG MACHINES

Joseph Haroutunian

1. The modern environment of machines and goods. 2. The influence of machines upon the minds of men: depersonalization. 3. The contemporary temper: ease, comfort, money. 4. Power among moderns: roots, manifestations and limitations. 5. Power, organization and their influence upon persons. 6. Machines, organization and the mass mind. 7. The center of the evil: organization, motives and coercion. 8. Specific instances: international relations, race, labor. 9. Conclusion. The internal contradictions of the machine age: reorganization and spiritual rebirth.

THE most influential factors in our lives are those of which we are hardly aware. Spectacular and exciting events like crime, painful disease, or war, are results of activity which we take for granted as integral to our existence. Hence it is not possible to deal with the evils in our midst without an understanding of their roots in our everyday life. The key to the solution of many a knotty problem in our time is to be sought not in its surface complications but in its roots in the more or less automatic behavior of men in their environment. It has therefore become absolutely necessary to discipline ourselves toward observing the obvious and commonplace facts which give rise to the all but desperate situations in social life today. The primary purpose of this essay is to contribute to our awareness of such facts and to the understanding of their power in our common life.

1. THE MODERN ENVIRONMENT

Any stable environment is one that contributes materially to our well-being. The world of sunshine, soil, growth, is necessary for our very existence. The world of machines and machine-made goods is necessary for the good of life as we know it. We can bear to be without some of our machine goods, but we should be lost without our total environment of technological skills and services. Our daily experience with machines includes a series of advantages which have become a part of us. What a contribution to ease and comfort is the electric light! What a time saver is the telephone! What an effort saver is the washing machine! And what a delight is the radio! The newspapers are a constant source of information and enlightenment. The family car makes for parties, outings, visits, shopping, trips. It makes movement swift, comfortable and enjoyable. Think of the benefits derived from cleaning fluids, canned or bottled foods, gas ranges, mechanical refrigeration, fountain pens, typewriters, threshing machines, and even the humble screw driver. One has only to walk through a grocery store, a hardware store, a drugstore, and a department store, in order to realize what a possibility of "abundant life" is provided by our new machine-made environment. Life without it is quite as unthinkable as life without air and water.

People enjoying machine products are "well-off." They are well-fed, well-dressed, well-housed and well-behaved. They are healthy and comfortable. They are neat, clean, free from smells except pleasant ones; with shiny teeth and glossy hair; and their skin is smooth. They are in general polite, reasonable and given to pleasant social intercourse. They are tolerant, men of good will, free from vulgarities and bitternesses which plague the lives of indigent people. They enjoy themselves variously—eating well, playing bridge, going to the movies, riding in their cars, reading the material pouring out of the press. Their superior status is well-attested by the fact that they arouse at once envy and servile attention from those wanting their "standard of life."

2. THE CONTEMPORARY MIND

The life of men with machines has profound influences upon their mind and character, and these influences have in turn serious consequences in our common life. The mind is formed by its contents. Minds preoccupied with things are repositories of images of those things and their operations. Such minds are things as ideas, and their workings correspond to the workings of things. They contemplate things, seek things, love things. Things are for them at once means of enjoyment and ends to be pursued. They themselves become instrumental to the acquisition of goods, and use others for the same end. They are loathe to allow irrelevant considerations to deter them from the pursuit of goods, and are severely tempted to give priority to any line of conduct which will enhance their possession and enjoyment. Friendships which do not contribute to their prosperity, especially those which impede their progress in acquisition, are sooner or later set aside, and alliances are formed which promise some new advantage in their pursuit of economic advancement.

Depe, sonalization

The most potent and common cause of depersonalization in modern life, with all its enormous consequences for the quality of our lives, is the re-formation of the human mind by its new content of ideas and ends derived from the new machine-made environment.

What do men think of? They think of things produced by machines. They have a radio. They want a car. A woman has an electric refrigerator. She wants a mechanical dishwasher. Men want money which is a symbol of things they and their wives can buy and enjoy. There is a constant *élan* for possession, and it finds expression in a multitude of images of machine products which fill up the mind. Minds filled and vitalized by images of things are impersonal in perspective, content and operation.

Reason itself is molded by mechanical processes and relations. It reflects cause and effect as seen in the operations of machines. It views the world as an indefinite number of mechanical sequences, in which fulfilled conditions yield desired ends. When the parts of a car are in good order and it is full of gas, one turns a key and steps on the starter, and the car goes ahumming. When the radio is out of order, one calls in an expert who "fixes it," and the thing functions again. The world consists of things, with specific mechanical organizations, responding to given sets of manipulation.

Our logic therefore is a reflection of machine processes, and our understanding a mirror of mechanical relations. Youth playing with airplanes or photography, men puttering with cars and radios, women preoccupied with cookbooks and gas ranges, are all unconsciously or consciously believers in sets of predetermined material orders, and arrange their existence accordingly.

Living automatically

Addiction to machines becomes as spontaneous and automatic as walking and eating. Without a certain discipline, men are prone to give themselves up to acquiring and using the goods in their environment. Farmers are preoccupied with sowing and reaping, merchants with buying and selling, men possessing machines with their construction and use. In every case it takes a special effort at self-criticism for a man to dissociate himself from his environment and to evaluate properly his relation with it. The easier way is simply to become a part of the environment, and to adjust oneself to it. Thus, a man is formed according to the things he uses. When dealing with organic material, he tends to act as an "organism." He reacts directly to cold and heat, to good food or bad, to security or insecurity with men and beasts. In dealing with machines, he is affected well or ill according to their availability, efficiency, productivity and servility. He is preoccupied with the running of his car or radio, with the use of his telephone or camera, with the advantages of can opener or electric switch. The fact that much of such preoccupation is almost automatic shows a man's integration into his mechanical environment and his genuine bondage to it.

Automatic relations are the most secure. They are immune to rational criticism, and determine the basic processes of life. So it is with digestion, imagination, heartbeat, breathing, etc. Such activities of the organism go on throughout life, and condition much of its behavior while it pursues the objects of its attention. The same is true in our machine environment. While we are wringing our hands about the grandiose social, economic and political problems of the day, our unconscious bondage to the machine and machine goods conditions the totality of our existence and produces its various effects of weal or woe without the benefit of reason or conscience. Much as bodily pains are symptoms of disease in the organism, so social suffering is evidence of illness in man in relation to his machine environment. Hence a radical treatment of social ills in our time without attention to the intercourse between man and machines is impossible.

3. THE TEMPER OF OUR TIME

The machine as such (which is an abstraction) is no more good or evil than nature as such (which is another abstraction). Both nature and machine are essential to our existence. They are sources of good for our lives. However, both are also sources of evil, or rather, are turned into evil by man. Hence the following discussion of evils in the lives of men with machines is no more an argument against machines than a discussion of organic diseases would be a denunciation of nature. Organic diseases are dealt with best by understanding the organism in relation to external nature. So our social diseases are dealt with best by understanding the relation of man to the environment of machines.

"Take thine ease"

Men with machines are confirmed lovers of *ease* and *comfort*. The advertisers of machines are never tired of describing their wares as conducive to easy and painless living. The easier it is to operate a machine and the more comfortable it makes one, the more excellent it is. As a matter of fact, nothing is praised so highly among us as painlessness. We are automatically drawn toward those who take away pain, and turn away from those who cause trouble. Pain has become evil simply considered. None but a fool of a schoolboy would prefer a hard lesson to one that is easy. None but a fool of a woman would prefer a recipe hard to convert into a dinner to one that is easy. None but a fool of a man would prefer a hard job to one that is easy. A hard bed is worse than a soft bed. Walking is worse than riding. Listening to the radio is easier and better than going to the concert hall. And going to the movies is better than going to the theater where one gets little without listening. Ease and comfort are good; difficulty, discomfort, pain, etc., are bad.

Money

The means of ease and comfort is money which enables us to acquire machines. Machines give us ease and make us comfortable, and machines are acquired with money. Money is therefore a prime good. Everybody wants money. Without money one can do nothing. Without money not even hospitals, churches or colleges can operate. Hence directors of hospitals, preachers in churches, presidents of colleges, not to mention businessmen, workers, farmers and other worldlings, are never so happy as when their institutions are on a "sound financial basis." It is assumed not only that without money one can do nothing, but also that with it everything can be done. Men with money, whether ministers or artists or shopkeepers, are superior men; poor men, farmers, workers or teachers, are inferior men.

Money today is a symbol of the Good, and to acquire money is to acquire the Good as to lose it is to lose the Good. There is no commandment greater than "Thou shalt acquire money." The most convincing sign of superiority among us is wealth. Sudden acquisition of "big money" is a very elating experience and penury is sheer spiritual devastation. Even those who by habit of life or thought are in general indifferent to pecuniary considerations, are strongly agitated when confronted with a large sum. The writer knows a man who will, all of a sudden, with no apparent reason, begin to murmur "one hundred thousand dollars," and keep on murmuring it until shocked into self-consciousness.

The love of money is perennial. It has been the despair of high-minded men ever since money appeared upon the earth. But the love of money today has qualities all its own. It is bound with a faith in money which goes with faith in machines. The assumed omnipotence of money is derived from the virtual omnipotence of machines in providing us with ease and comfort. The machines have opened indefinite possibilities of acquisition and enjoyment. And money, which symbolizes machine power, is a promise of indefinite progress in acquisition and enjoyment. Money today can do things impossible previous to the machine age. It can provide us with goods which were impossible without the machine. Hence the love of money is a distillation of the loves for all the benefits provided and promised by machines. Hence also the love of money is intensified and absolutized in a way peculiar to life in this environment of machines. The more one can enjoy with money, the more one loves money. The more people can enjoy things through money, the more people love money. Hence, more people love money more in a machine environment than in one where goods are bounded within natural limits.

4. A NEW LOVE OF POWER

The love of money is the love of comfort and ease. It is also the love of power. The pursuit of money cannot be identified simply with the pursuit of things useful and pleasurable.

Neither the utilitarian desire for the "greatest good for the greatest number," nor the hedonist emphasis upon pleasure, so common and misleading among us, can explain the lust for money even at the expense of pleasure. People are tempted to sacrifice health, peace, leisure and "good times" for the sake of becoming men of power in the several fields of enterprise.

It is more gratifying to be at the head of an organization (financial, educational or ecclesiastical), than to live without power, even if with comfort. People will work themselves into ill-health and even death in order to attain and retain positions of authority and dictatorship. They are never so happy as when they can tell someone "what to do" and when they feel that nobody can tell *them* "where to get off." It is intolerable not to to able to impose one's will upon anyone, and it is absolutely self-realizing to reckon that one's will is law in a given organization of human relations. It is good to be a lord in one's household. It is wonderful to be official or unofficial lord in a store, factory, town or church. The bigger the store, factory, town, or church, the more gratifying it is to be a lord over it.

The more power is represented by an institution in which one is lord, the more powerful is the lord, and the more he is gratified. The lords of billion-dollar financial or industrial organizations are mighty great lords. Head men in the bureaucracy of a powerful nation are a little less mighty great lords. Bishops, presidents, superintendents, heads, editors, managers, directors, trustees, leaders, foremen, executives, generals, sergeants, professors and a host of variegated bosses, constitute a conglomeration of half-divinities whose behavior is unintelligible apart from universal and primary love of power over men and things. There is hardly a corner of the modern world where little Napoleons are not contending for power. There is hardly a man, however simple, to whom power is not sour rather than bad grapes. There is hardly a soul who is not uneasy because he is not Lord God Almighty. A nisus toward infinite power belongs to the structure of the human spirit, and little is understood without an acknowledgment of it.

Limitation of power

The more power is available, the more intense is the search for it. The more uncontested the power possessed, the more it is refused to anyone who reaches for it. Hence, in this age of machines, where power is reckoned in terms of machines with millions of horsepower, more servile than the weakest horse, the power motif in human life is indefinitely emphasized.

The story in chapter three of Genesis makes it plain that man's "natural" desire is for life first and for power secondly. When Adam sinned, he lived a life of hard labor and died, presumably much earlier than proposed by Providence. What he lost was Life, a decent and peaceful life, rather than omnipotence. The story of Adam is an edifying discourse to the effect that it is well to live within the limits set by the Creator. While men of limited power lived vis-à-vis nature, it seemed sensible to live by the favor of nature's omnipotent God, rather than to aspire toward His sovereignty. They wanted power for the sake of a good life in nature, in obedience to God. Power beyond that, as sought by the men who built the Tower of Babel, was considered sinful and destructive. Later on it was told that a prince among angels was hurled from heaven to hell because he lusted for the power of God. Man's spirit has always lusted for infinite power. But his life in nature "put brakes" on that lust, and recommended a decent, prolonged life instead. Men preferred "eternal life" to "infinite power."

Today the situation of man is different. He is not aware of any serious concern with eternity. He hardly expects "immortality," and is not deeply concerned about the matter. It is debatable as to whether unbelief or unconcern comes first. However, it is true that men care more for power than for life. In other words, it is *infinity* rather than *eternity* that captivates the human soul today. And this infinity is actually a steady impulse toward the indefinite multiplication of power as conditioned by the machines and their organizations. The perennial concern with eternity and the related infinity, have been deeply qualified by a concern with an infinity without eternity, an infinity approximated by the increase of mechanical power and its various symbols. It seems needless to add that an understanding of the modern mind and much more, a genuine improvement of its condition, were impossible without a thorough analysis of the new impulse toward infinity as stated above. The proposed cures for the ills of our time may well be ineffective so long as the spiritual revolution in our machine-made society is left out of the calculations of would-be benefactors of mankind. Humanly speaking, it has become necessary that religious leaders turn their concentrated and persistent attention to the spirit of man with machines, and understand it in a way comparable to the classic, traditional analyses of human nature as known in the historical theologies of the Christian Church. This is a task which can no longer be left to accident and incident without making the work of the Church today peripheral and powerless.

5. ORGANIZATION FOR POWER

However, the new double impulse toward ease and power is constantly vitalized by the objective situation of men. It is not possible to understand human nature today apart from the social organizations in which men exist. The overwhelming

drives toward possession and power in our time have counter-
parts in technological, economic, political and sundry organizations, which bind men all the more securely because men are
bound to them voluntarily and even unconsciously. The power
after which men lust is organized power, the power of systems,
of banks and factories, and transportation, and chainstores,
and the combinations of them. Power today is acquired through
organization: organization for the accumulation of capital and
for the co-operations in an automobile or shoe factory; organization for the acquisition of raw materials, for transportation,
for sale; organization for bargaining and coercion; organization for the control of political power and for the molding of
the public mind. Without organization there is no power. With
organization there is an indefinite multiplication of it. Hence
the seeker after power, that is, the modern man, is a profound
and confirmed believer in organization. He can do all things by
organization.

Organization in our society is of money, machines and men.
It is essentially an organization of things. The men in an organization of things function as things. In modern organizations all
things are measured in terms of certain units: of money, or
energy, or size, or some physical quality such as color, material
or form. The primary purpose of organization is to make profit
through more production, better production, less cost in production, control of prices, manipulation of capital, effective
advertising, etc. The matter can be put differently. The purpose
of organization is the service of the public through the various
means suggested above. Modern organization, however, is essentially an organization of things and their symbols. It is a
rationalized affair, a product of calculation, utilizing human
energies in so far as these contribute to the making of power
conditioned by machinery.

Organizations and persons

Contemporary social organizations are for certain limited purposes, e.g., for the accumulation of capital or the transportation of men and goods. Men as well as machines are important in so far as they perform certain specific and limited functions. Some are salesmen, some are conductors; others are clerks in charge of files, others elevator men. Each man has his job, and he is recognized and estimated by it. A man is one who plays this or that role in an organization far greater than himself. The job defines men's *raison d'être*, and apart from the job he is without value. His private life, his sensibilities and responses, his own personal destiny as well as responsible decisions, as unrelated to his job, are secondary even when consequential. He is a functioning part first, a *person* secondly. He is qualified and disqualified as an instrument rather than as an end. And since his livelihood and security depend upon his job, sooner or later he learns to evaluate himself in terms of it, and becomes so absorbed by it as to minimize his unique existence as a person. Thus he is induced, perhaps subtly and yet overwhelmingly, to regard himself as he is regarded by the organization: as boss, worker, salesman, clerk, teacher, etc., simply considered. Thus the organization depersonalizes the man, and coerces him voluntarily to forego his freedom. The better adjusted a man is to his job, the more he is likely to be an unfree or impersonal entity.

The nature of contemporary organization makes personality irrelevant. Moreover, the sheer size of such organization is like that of a vast, immovable thing. When hundreds, and thousands, of men, through millions of invested capital, together with systems of machinery, with thousands of horsepower energy, form an organization, each man is actually a small part of a great big complex of things. He is very small, and impotent against the whole of which he is a part. His private ends are no match for the public ends of the organization. There may be aspects to his existence, such as his family affairs, which are irrelevant to the organization: but he does not transcend the organization in any way that will enable him to subordinate it to his personal life. Hence he is essentially not a person, because a person is one with power to subordinate all things to one's judgment of truth and right. This is perhaps the major source of anxiety in modern life.

The mind of a part of an organization is the pattern of the organization itself. The part is the part of a whole, and as such reflects the whole. Hence it is that a man with a job in an organization identifies his good with the good of the organization. He feels secure when the organization is running well and his job remains an ongoing function in it. He may be critical of certain frictions in the moving machinery of which he is part, but he has no perspective from which he may criticize the organization as such. Hence his judgments are at the mercy of the organization or rather, of the thinkers in the organization. He finds it sensible to think as he is led to think, and thinks like the other equivalent parts in the organization. Freedom of thought, that is thought itself, is never too conspicuous among job holders. Even where there are conflicting interests in an organization, as is often the case, there are several levels of mass mind, rather than a noticeable plurality of thinkers.

The existence of a part is extremely precarious without the whole. In fact, a part, like the wheel of a car, without the whole, is a lost thing. It is really not itself any more. It is not that the part, as a wheel without the car, is not really a wheel. The wheel, for full existence, is absolutely dependent upon the car. So the man as a job holder is *absolutely dependent* upon the organization. A man who lives in a given organization so that he is a part of it, and of nothing else in a way necessary for existence, is absolutely dependent upon that organization, no matter in how many other relations he exists. Hence in spite of the multiplicity of social relations, in families, clubs, churches, etc., men live in absolute dependence upon organizations in which they are job holders. And such dependence is not conducive to critical, creative, personal existence. Even functionaries in educational and ecclesiastical organizations are not always given to personal existence as thought of in this paper.

The dependence of men upon organizations is established and confirmed by the fact that it is today impossible to think of the good life apart from power, privilege and goods, which are available only through organization. The measure of the dependence of men upon the institutions of society is the measure of their attachment to the goods which the latter provide. Men who "cannot live without" telephones, electric lights, radios and cars, are in fact absolutely dependent upon the industries that produce them. They are in bondage to the orders and systems in our society which provide them with these things necessary for their existence today. Thus their bondage is all the firmer because it is unrecognized and unappreciated, because it has become natural and automatic. Hence those who enjoy a goodly portion of the advantages provided by their environment are determined to perpetuate its present constitution, and are willing servants of the powers in control. The order of society today is no less sacrosanct to them than was "the order of nature" to those who lived under it. In both cases we have a bondage of man to his environment and a necessity that he be delivered from it lest he lose his soul.

6. THE MASS MIND

Now we are ready to look into the "mind of the masses" as formed in our time. First of all we must set aside the error that the mass mind belongs to a particular group in our society. Everyone likes to think that he is not one of the masses. People who read and write about the masses are constantly moved to find them among the less literate, the poor, the factory workers, semi-slum dwellers, and the like. Every other man who lives on a salary and lives in a suburb is disquieted by a vision of men with dirty clothes and drawn faces who are set to deprive him of car, home and the "Sunday Times." He is made anxious by the well-advertised possibility that crowds of ignorant, vulgar and violent people will one day push aside the present hierarchy of privilege and reduce him to their present level of penury and deprivation. Thus clerks and college students, preachers and other professionals, businessmen, farmers and entertainers; middle-class churchgoers, bridge players, those who eat at the better restaurants and read on the advices of "the book-of-the-month club"; all bearers of morality and culture, live oppressed by a Presence, the presence of the nebulous "masses" and recoil from it as from something tainted and indecent.

Who are "the masses"?

The common notion of the masses is a product of one type of mass mind. The identification of "the masses" vaguely with "the lower classes," with foreigners, workers, racial minorities, is a device whereby those with special and often undeserved privileges justify themselves to themselves. This reaction to "the masses" is itself an evidence of a mass mind induced by the present organization of society.

The discussion in this paper so far leads us to an analysis of the mass mind quite different from the one mentioned above. The masses appear wherever the mind of the individual is a simple reflection of the pattern of an organization. When men behave automatically as parts of an organization, when they accept the good of an organization as the good absolutely, when they conceive their good in terms of the good produced by the organization, when they think, value, will, feel, act, in manners dictated by the organization—then they belong to a mass. When men's judgments are molded by a given newspaper, or advertiser, or radio commentator, or by the higher-ups in an organization, then they belong to the masses. When they reflect the prejudices, tastes, standards, ambitions and responses of a group, they are parts of a mass. The mass is constituted neither by men of low income nor by hardy men in overalls. It is a group in which private judgment is suspended. And such groups cut crisscross through the length and breadth of society. It is likely to appear among the privileged for one reason and among the unprivileged for another. The former think according to their advantages in an organization; the latter think less subtly in terms of their disadvantages. But both think of advantages in relation to an organization, and have notions identical with a multitude in their particular situation. The mass man is one who does not think his own thoughts. He is everywhere, in every stratum of our society, occupied with any job or profession. An awareness of the ubiquity of the mass man today is indispensable for proper dealings with him. In fact a recognition of oneself as mass man Number One is indispensable for effective wrestling with this terrifying monster of our time.

Organization and the masses

The emergence of the masses today is incomprehensible apart from the new significance of organization. The elementary fact in our society is that the goods men seek are acquired through participation in organized groups. Power, privilege, pleasure, possession, are in and through organizations. Individuals, by themselves, are unable to make any appreciable impression upon the social processes of our time. Nothing much can be accomplished in business, or politics, or education, or religion, except by setting in motion forces issuing from the interests and will of organized groups of men. Anyone seeking to "get somewhere" must work in committees, commissions, societies, conferences, leagues, lobbies, bureaus, associations, unions, chambers, clubs, assemblies and conventions. He must identify his interests with those of a fairly large body of men. He must think their thoughts and act in unison with them. He must be ambitious without being self-critical, and press for common objectives which define his desires rather than his worth.

The mass man is essentially irresponsible. His attention is riveted upon what he can get by his participation in a group. He imposes no duty upon himself other than one made necessary by his life in the group. He acts in the group without assuming responsibility for the consequences of group action. If good comes, he takes credit. If evil comes, he denies having done it. Success and failure are essentially amoral; they are objective situations, due to reasons of group power and strategy. The mass man is no longer a person. He is a seat of desire for available goods and advantages.

The mass man believes in group action. He is happy when a large number of men share his intentions and set out to fulfill them. If he is a worker, he becomes a union member. If he is a farmer, he joins a farm bureau or bloc. If he is a businessman, he is in the chamber of commerce. If he is a clergyman, he joins the ministerial association. If he is a statesman, he is for alliances, leagues and unions. He is concerned more with objectives than with motives and moral congruities between worth and intention. He himself is no problem. He is busy with problems. His attention is always turned outward, to a social situation. He is incapable of a serious consideration of his own spirit, and avoids meeting it as though it were a dangerous monster, which it may be. The mass man, whether factory worker, or journalist, or sociologist, or parson, is a being attached to the blessings provided by machines, and seeks them through concerted action with beings like himself. Such mass mentality is ubiquitous today, and may well be the undoing of many a proposed scheme toward the Good Society.

7. THE CENTER OF EVIL

At given levels such mass mentality is proper and unblameworthy enough. If machine society makes organization and group action necessary, there is not much use in fearing or bewailing the fact. Organization is as inevitable today as individualism was among frontiersmen a hundred years ago. Besides, it is necessary for our existence as Americans. Without it the fission of the atom's nucleus, and a hundred lesser performances of modern science and technology would have been impossible. Society today is a conglomeration of organizations. Hence, labor, industry, artists, Negroes, clergymen—all of them organize. Otherwise they become ineffective in our society. And they obtain their several objectives which are usually legitimate in view of present possibilities, through organization. Organization is good, and is here to stay and to condition larger segments of our existence.

At the same time, it is not possible to understand our times without seeing how minds reflecting organizations are sources of terrible evils and possibilities of future evils.

Organization, motives, and conflict

Men organize in order to derive maximum advantages in our
machine civilization. Directly or indirectly, most organizations
are for the sake or giving those organized a maximum share in
the wealth and power available because of machines. Let alone
business and political organizations, how long would men's
clubs and colleges continue were it not believed that in them
there is chance for advantage in making money? The position
of the churches is rather ambiguous. They seem to have some
therapeutic value. However, good churchmanship often pays
social-economic as well as "spiritual" dividends.

Groups organized for certain primary objectives will sacrifice
lesser goods for the sake of the greatest. Bankers seeking maximum return for money invested, watch above all the difference
between output and income in given enterprises. They are interested in their investors, and their own profit. The "captains of
industry" want profit through a high differential between cost
and price, and through a large sale list. They also want to be
the masters of the situation in their factories and related enterprises. They want to keep and augment their power. Workers,
on the other hand, want steady jobs, good pay, shorter hours,
better working conditions and the power of partners. Clerks,
salesmen, lesser managers and the like, considering themselves
better off than the workers, appropriate the point of view of the
"big bosses" and usually become the instruments of "management."

Now, in such a conflict of interests, the last resort is *coercion.*
A group is a seat of power, and uses its power in order to attain
its own special objectives. It relies on power, seeks power, uses
power. In this process, it uses the forms of power available to it:
the power of the state, or of capital, or of skill, or of arms, or

of public opinion. In any case, it presents a threat of physical coercion. Groups are organized for exercising mass force. The use of such force is inherent in their formation and existence. Hence the mass mind of a member of an organized group is directed toward successful coercion. Hence, also, coercion appears and reappears in modern society in spite of multitudes of men who dislike it. It is true that in many instances conflicts among groups are mitigated and averted through arbitration and compromise. No group exists purely for the sake of power, and men in groups will reason for the sake of peace, security and the enjoyment of goods. Thus men use power with calculation. Nevertheless, the use of force for the attainment of mass objectives is a constant possibility issuing in recurrent action. The blindness to be avoided is that coercion by mass minds is incidental and accidental. The professed peaceful proclivities of mass-minded men, expressed in universal desire for peace and prosperity, must not lull us to the assumption that the conflicts in contemporary society are mere aberrations. Otherwise one shall understand little and can do little more than be continually surprised by the inhumanities of men of good will overrunning the world. In the context of our society, impulses toward power, privileges and enjoyment of goods, are primary even though not always explicit. And unless such impulses are acknowledged in ourselves and dealt with as deadly possibilities, there will be no meeting with truth in our situation, and hence no meeting with God.

8. SPECIFIC INSTANCES

The nations

The social evils of our time are products of the mass mind, and the mass mind, our mind, has no cure for them. International rivalry is a notorious instance. What is the essence of nationalism today? Is it not the desire of peoples making up nations to acquire or retain technological advantages which will give them power, security and a "high standard of living"? What American, or Englishman, or Russian, or Frenchman, will deny the desire in him to see himself and the people of his nationality in possession of the power and prosperity promised by machines? Any politician can move men to enthusiasm by informing them that his primary concern is their peace, power and prosperity. Here is a mass mind that is fast becoming universal, and will inevitably spread into the other continents together with the spread of machines. It is this mind that has made for the frequency and intensification of wars in our time, and probably war in the future cannot be averted without a profound conversion of this mass mind. Journalists and publicists hope that the advantages of international co-operation, and now the sheer threat of the "atomic bomb," will induce nations to live together in peace. We need no radical criticism of the modern mind, no change of perspective and intention, no reorientation toward existence in the machine world; no personal conversion of journalists, publicists, industrialists, workers, preachers. No, let us retain the mass mind of our time. Let us only organize for peace. Let us pursue the ideal of world prosperity. Let us think of ways and means of removing the several obstacles in the way of international understanding, etc. And now, let us fear "the atomic bomb"!

We do not know how far the publicists and putterers will succeed in averting another disaster. But it does seem that a peace maintained without uncovering the roots of conflict in the mass mind formed by mechanical organization, with its reliance on manipulation and rearrangement, is precarious. Nothing is needed more today than a capacity to transcend this universal mass mind of our time. Whether we the Christians are capable of such a prodigious feat remains to be seen. Maybe we must first see how incapable we are of it.

The races

The race problem is a bewilderingly vast and complex matter. When we consider the historical dimensions of the relations between Jews and Gentiles, Negroes and whites, Asiatics and Westerners, we are certainly impressed with the tangle of problems which evoke despair and paralysis. Here also, however, understanding and fruitful action are usually excluded by our subjection to the mass mind of our time. Here also, advocates of justice and brotherhood are in the habit of viewing race conflict as a problem in every sphere but that of the machine mentality common to all of us. They propose that Jews and Gentiles live together in peace and share the common blessings of the machine age. They propose that Negroes be given opportunity equal to that of the whites for "Life, Liberty and the pursuit of Happiness." They propose that Western nations share their technical knowledge and skills with the Asiatics, and bring prosperity to the "backward" people in the East. In short, the problem of race relations becomes usually one of sharing our advantages with those who are without them. It is argued positively that when this is done theré will be one world of peace and prosperity; and negatively that otherwise there will be bigger wars and Western civilization will explode away. The reasonableness of such arguments is obvious, but they ignore the nisus for infinite power in the mass mind today. They ignore that the race between predatory and hedonistic impulses among us is a neck and neck affair. Therefore they have no means of slowing the pace of predacity which is headed toward ruin.

The race problems assume another aspect when a man examines his own relations to Jews, Negroes or Asiatics, and when the latter in their turn do the same. The truth is that the white Gentile is constantly overwhelmed by a "race consciousness" over which he has little control. Try as he may, and many do try, he is unable to think of a man as a man first, and a Jew, or Negro, or Chinese, secondly. His very acknowledgment of virtues in other races in general and in certain members of another race in particular, reveals an incapacity to overcome his sense of otherness from them. It is this sense which reveals the mass man in him and underlies his apparently unintelligible failures to treat men of other races according to his reason and conscience. Perennial race consciousness among tribes and peoples is a function of groups in search for power. Race consciousness in our times is qualified, established and intensified by the nature and extent of power available in our civilization of abundant machine goods.

It is unreasonable to expect that there will be any palpable diminution of race conflict without a radical reorientation of the mass mind, both in content and operation, which is integral to our civilization, and therefore common to the several "races" involved in it. Even while much is said and done toward racial fraternity, no sensible man can escape the suspicion that we may not avert race conflict sufficiently and soon enough to avoid future holocausts. While this suspicion lasts, it is only sensible to study the roots of race tension in our own spirits as reflecting the mind of our day. It is not promised that we shall thus solve the race problem. But one must insist that only thus shall we understand ourselves better, and meet the judgment and mercy of God.

Labor

A discussion of the mass mind without reference to "the labor movement" would be incomplete. According to common preju-

dices (among those who do not work with factory machines),
the masses today are multitudes of factory workers who seem
bent upon more pay, more security, greater share in goods and
pleasures, and more power.

But it takes a great deal of foolishness to regard the behavior
of the workers as due to a peculiar failure in virtue. The workers
are fighting against a tradition of exploitation which the possibilities of well-being offered by the very machines they use
make unbearable. The machines are, as it were, constantly
boasting of "the American standard of living" they offer to the
people. Think of what a man can have these days, of the ease
and leisure he may enjoy, of the security and health and freedom he may have! Wherever the machines reign, they convince
the total mind of the people, including the minds of workers, that
the good of life is the goods they provide. Therefore it is nothing
less than inevitable that workers should seek all the advantages
available in our society; that they should rebel against unemployment, slums, insecurity, poverty, unfreedom and their
hundred teeth which grind the faces of their families as well as
their own; that they should form unions which enable them to
approach the powerful with power; that they should form mass
minds identical with those of the privileged except in the
knowledge of being unprivileged; that they should lust without
limit for the limitless powers and goods produced by machines.
The workers share the mind of the age as do their employers.

If the workers look more massy than the rest of us it is because they need to act in a mass more than those whose power is
embedded in law and tradition. If they are more crude and
masslike it is not necessary to regard them as other than mere
men working with a tempo and rhythm which are mechanical
rather than human. It is not within the general range of human
resistance to become accessory to our assembly lines and relent-

less machines without suffering physical and mental disintegration. And if workers show evidences of "the mass mind" in the ordinary sense, if they resort to coercion of various forms while restive with less than they can get, it is well to recognize that they exhibit one particular manifestation of the social mind in its essential drive for power and goods. Thus "the labor problems" of our day appear as one facet of the total problem of existence in the machine age: the problem of the mass mind in a society organized around the power machines.

Numerous men of knowledge and good will are engaged in trying to bring peace into the present scene of tension and strife in our economic life. Labor leaders, industrialists, businessmen, statesmen, journalists, economists, sociologists, moralists, educators and churchmen recognize the gravity of the situation in these times of "reconversion" and world unrest. Proposals, each one sensible and all debatable, pour from presses and consultation rooms. Doubtless much misery and conflict can be and may be averted through the concerted labors of experts. And it is the political duty of us all to give encouragement to any activity promising maximum justice and peace in our economic institutions.

Nevertheless, it is the thesis of this essay that structural and functional adjustments, and the compromises involved in effecting them may well be insufficient to avert future disasters for long. The present conflicts between labor and management, although occasioned by the difficulties of transition from a war to a peace economy, are not simply occasional. Economic struggle has been too persistent in our age, and its tempo has been growing much too steadily, for anyone to assume that it is incidental to our civilization. It has been reduced and eliminated in totalitarian countries by sheer force of arms. It will not be reduced enough, or eliminated, in free countries without the emergence of a critical self-knowledge and a radical change in men among machines.

9. CONCLUSION

Internal contradictions

The desperate difficulties in the large-scale problems mentioned above arise, at one level, from their size and complexity. It is a fact that we have unwittingly produced organizational monsters which we have neither the wit nor the strength to subjugate. It is quite a question as to whether human intelligence can deal with the organizational hydra strangling us.

On the other hand, the lack of intelligence is not our only misfortune. When brains which split atoms act as though incapable of organizing for peace and prosperity, one must look for reasons other than mere weakness in the "gray cells." Not even "social inertia," "cultural lag," "psychological maladjustment," etc., real as they are, explain the frustration of man in the world today. It is as though the machinery of life today produced its own monkey wrench and broke down its own arm or axle. The social process looks like machinery with contradictory parts, making life itself a contradiction.

And so it is. Our technological society suffers from an internal contradiction. It is full of promises of ease, freedom, opportunity, progress and indefinite power; while the men in it are ill at ease, dependent, "stuck to a job," stationary and weak. The people are promised abundance, and many of them are oppressed by their limited existence. They are promised leisure and enjoyment, yet they must push until too weary to enjoy even their food. They are supposed to be carefree and secure, and they are overwhelmed with anxiety before an unpredictable future. They are supposed to live in peace, and they are living under a dark shadow of threatenings. There is a permanent contradiction between promise and fulfillment. The promise glows with the light of infinity; the fact is a dull gray of unrealized hopes. The very goods men possess are turned into things of indifference because of their anxiety and frustration. We are actually lost men, whose primary comfort is blaming someone else for our discomfiture.

Hence, we are enemies of anyone who is weaker than ourselves, and approach all men with caution. At best, we divert ourselves by seeking a way of escape through organization! In the meanwhile, the contradiction of the finite and the infinite in our minds continues to turn our efforts into failures, and new seeds of conflict are sown in our souls. Such is the spiritual structure in our society of man with machines. It is needless to add that such structure cannot function without friction and danger of breakdown. It is needless also to add that an organization of such men cannot constitute a peaceful society.

Reorganization and rebirth

It has been claimed that the above contradictions will disappear with a proper organization of social relations. But how are we to organize so that the machines will not produce the contradictory loves for power and enjoyment, for autonomy and security, for prosperity and domination? And while these contradictions remain in the human soul, how are we to organize for peace, as against predacity and warfare?

Publicists who are concerned with the problems of "the good society" are busy making plans and devising means, while they seldom cast a critical eye upon the motives and objectives which dominate their efforts. Their subjection to the mass mind inspired by machines is evident in their pious assumption that world-wide peace and prosperity are the ultimate "desire of the nations." The real question for them is: How shall we arrange and organize for common happiness with machines and their products? Arrange and organize! For common happiness! Such are the slogans of machine-made minds.

Organization is essential to our society. The machines must be organized in order to produce the goods without which we are not willing to live. Industrial organization requires banks and investment houses, transportation systems, companies and corporations, chain and department stores. Such powerful institutions encourage the organization of workers and farmers, and necessitate political institutions which shall work for the good of society at large. Sooner or later every group representing a particular interest—religious, racial, professional—becomes organized. Thus we confront a multitude of organizations in which individuals seek to further their power and privilege in the community.

There is no use bewailing such a state of affairs. It simply is a fact that democracy today requires a multiplicity of organizations none of which shall be too powerful. The peace of the world requires organizations on various levels, and a balance of power among them. Peace among races requires organization among minorities and power sufficient for resisting oppression and exploitation. There cannot be justice or order in our time without organization and greater integration of organized groups. So all success to those who work toward organizing the present conglomeration of conflicting forces into "one world." And we must join them.

However, if there is any truth in the thesis of this essay, organization of groups constituted today will produce no telling and lasting results. We must learn to become critical of the mass mind today which believes that sufficient cleverness at organization can solve the pressing problems of the day. We need a new understanding of men among machines who, after all, are responsible for the sickness of our time. We must comprehend the way in which "decent, ordinary human beings," engaged in the pursuit of the goods available in our time, are led to engage in perilous conflict with their fellow men. We must see how it is that Americans, Russians and Englishmen, who are so eager for peace and prosperity, manage to provoke one another to dangerous rivalries. We need to understand the reasons for terrifying tensions among good Jews and good Gentiles, good Negroes and good whites, and the incredible irrationalities which play havoc with our best intentions. In short, we need a radically new insight into the spirit of "man among machines" who falls into evil as sparks fly upwards.

And where shall we look for such an insight if not among Christians who follow a Master whose "kingdom is not of this world"? Where shall we find the self-transcendence necessary for self-knowledge but among Christians whose religion concerns man's ultimate destiny? The Christians have an indispensable first task to perform in our generation: and that task is to contribute to a proper self-knowledge among men with machines, a self-knowledge without which there can be no organization capable of forming a society of men and women living together in decent justice and peace.

FURTHER READING

CHASE, STUART. *Men and Machines.* New York: The Macmillan Company, 1929.

MITCHELL, WESLEY C., ed. *What Veblen Taught.* New York: The Viking Press, 1936.

MUMFORD, LEWIS. *Technics and Civilization*. New York: Harcourt, Brace and Company, Inc., 1934.

RUSSELL, BERTRAND. *Power*. New York: W. W. Norton & Company, Inc., 1938.

THOMAS, C. W., ed. *Essays in Contemporary Civilization*. New York: The Macmillan Company, 1931.

3

RIVALRIES FOR POWER

Elmer J. F. Arndt

1. The extent of power rivalries. 2. Political rivalries: the drive to expansion and the contribution of nationalism and science; conflict and the effect of total war; power and international co-operation. 3. The relationship between political and economic power; the function of democracy. 4. Economic rivalries: corporations, cartels, trade associations and responsibility for economic power; the labor movement and concentration of economic power. 5. Rivalries for public opinion: the importance of public opinion and its control; the two dominant rivals and their forms in the United States; religious rivalry. 6. The problem and the challenge: the limitations of power on the individual; the use of power.

---

1. THE EXTENT OF POWER RIVALRIES

THE preceding paper makes clear the fact that human society is the arena in which the struggle for power is waged and that its organization is determined by the outcome of the struggle. This fact is significant not only for understanding the organization of society but also for social ethics. For the degree of justice achievable within the nation or within the world depends upon the distribution of power and the kinds of power distributed.

The moral quality of the lives of men, classes and nations is expressed in the purposes for which power is exercised. It is practically impossible to overstate the significance of the power rivalries of the contemporary world, either for understanding the modern scene or for preserving and enhancing those values which are comprised under the word "civilization."

With the discovery of the means of atomic fission, a tremendous physical power is at hand. Its availability for military purposes has posed an issue of life or death, making world organization for establishing justice and maintaining peace a necessity if civilization is to avoid destruction. Its potential availability for constructive purposes has no less far-reaching consequences and likewise makes new demands on the human spirit.

For the United States—as well as for other democratic nations—the new forms of magnitude of economic power raise issues of fundamental import: the fate of political democracy and the fate of democratic values. The power of propaganda, enhanced by technical means, such as press and radio, and guided by psychological knowledge, opens a new dimension in the control of human life which extends to the mind and spirit of man. The very existence of the individual, his material welfare, his social relations and his spiritual life are vitally involved in contemporary power rivalries and their outcome.

Power in human relationships is usually regarded as the ability of individuals or groups to impose their will upon other individuals or groups. Those who can compel others to do as they wish them to do and who can prevent others from interfering with their own desires possess power. Such power is generally exercised by force. Moral suasion is not regarded as power in this sense, since it leaves the one to whom it is directed free to accept or to reject its offices. Power implies that ability to coerce is always present although not always used.

The desire for such ability to dominate others is deeply rooted in human nature. It is one of man's chief desires. It may spring from a desire for recognition or from a desire for security or from a desire to overcome the limits of human life. Whatever its basic motivation may be, its presence in group relationships throughout history cannot be gainsaid. People have not been content simply to control nature; they have sought to control each other.

There are many forms of power. Bertrand Russell in his book *Power* speaks of direct physical power over the body exercised by such organizations as the army and the police; the power of propaganda and education exercised by schools, churches and political parties; the power of rewards and punishments used by economic organizations. Power rivalries are all-pervasive: rivalries between nations, between races, between management and labor, between corporations, between social institutions, between political parties, between sectional interests, between urban and rural areas, and between individuals for positions of power.

The present discussion will be limited to pointing out some significant power rivalries. We shall, for the most part, be dealing with the import of three forms of power: political, economic and propaganda power.

2. POWER RIVALRIES: POLITICAL

The drive for expansion

Every state tends to seek an indefinite expansion of its power. Expansion is limited generally only by the quantity of power the state possesses, which is to say, primarily by the power of other states to resist the expansion. This tendency of states to extend their political domination is abundantly illustrated in history. Persia sought to extend its sovereignty over Greece; Athens, having defeated the Persians, sought to extend her domination over the Greeks even to the extent of including Sicily in her empire; Rome's expansion included the whole Mediterranean area; under Napoleon, France sought the hegemony of Europe; only yesterday Germany sought to win for herself world domination and Japan the domination of the vast territories and teeming peoples of East Asia; with the victory of the United Nations, the rivalry for power between the great powers (subordinated during the war) at once emerges and threatens the unity achieved for the waging of the war. The United States, though disclaiming any territorial ambitions, demands unqualified control of strategic bases in the Pacific taken from Japan; though committed to world organization, is urged by responsible men to keep the secret of the atomic bomb and to embark on a program of peacetime compulsory military training—measures which, however justified on other grounds, contribute to the maintenance of her dominant power.[1] That these policies are advocated in the name of defense with

[1] President Truman has expressed the view that the secret of the atomic bomb should be kept and recommended compulsory peacetime military training. At the time of writing (March, 1946), it appears that the United States, Great Britain and Canada have adopted the policy that the atomic bomb secret will not be disclosed until adequate safeguards are devised for the control of atomic energy. (Meanwhile the United States continues the manufacture of atomic bombs.) The present issue in Congress is over the question whether the control of atomic energy shall be in civilian or military hands, and, if the former, the extent of civilian control. The Congress has not yet acted at this time on compulsory peacetime military training, although such a measure has had the support of the Executive, the State, War and Navy Departments, and many organizations and influential individuals.

explicit disavowals of any aggressive purpose may justify them in American eyes but hardly obtains their complacent acceptance by other powers, great and small, who have had experience with the order and justice our power has imposed on them. The important fact is that the proposals for preserving the power dominance of the United States are based upon the premise that there are other states or combinations of states which would welcome the opportunity not merely to limit our freedom of action but to expand their own power at our expense. Rivalry for power is the framework within which the state strives to maintain its existence.

The rivalry for power between states is not only political but economic as well. The struggle for control of natural resources —oil, for example—the struggle for control of markets and the struggle for control of communications and transportation are too well known to require extended treatment. Political imperialism may go hand in hand with economic imperialism or the two may be divorced from each other. The British and Dutch empires illustrate their union; the United States has not found it necessary, with important exceptions, to impose political domination on other peoples to secure her economic aims.

The expansive tendencies of states, which are at the root of the struggle for power, are a compound of their vitality and their moral pretensions. Their vitality expresses itself in dissatisfaction with control restricted to the national boundaries and their moral pretensions are made justifications of their egoism. States claim for themselves a civilizing mission (as Italy did in justification of its attack on Ethiopia), or liberation from a foreign yoke (as Japan did in justification of her war in East Asia), or preservation of civilization against a threatening menace (as Hitler did with such astonishing success with his claim to be a bulwark against Bolshevism).

Nationalism and science

The egoism of states has not been produced, but it has been nurtured and implemented by two modern developments: the rise of nationalism and the development of science. Nationalism, in its unmitigated form, absolutizes the nation thus denying the unity of humanity. Its exclusiveness and its subordination of human values to the values of nationality defy the spiritual unity of mankind. It is a tribalistic religion which makes the national state the supreme object of loyalty and the source of the meaning of life for its citizens. The pretension to absoluteness, characteristic of nationalism, unites its citizens in uncritical devotion to the nation and provides a spiritual dynamic for the conquest of others. Professor Hocking writes:

> The national impulse, as it ripens, is not destined to be satisfied with a local self-determination. With maturity, the impulse will always arrive to give advice, to administer beyond its borders, to imagine itself a universal empire.[2]

The logic of nationalism ends in war for mastery—cultural as well as political and economic mastery—over others who have the misfortune to belong to a different, and therefore inferior, nation. How terrible a fate awaits weak nations threatened by a strong one imbued with an unqualified nationalistic spirit has been revealed by the treatment of the countries occupied by Germany before her defeat. The terrible thing about the imperialism of pure nationalism is that its aim is not the unification of peoples in a spiritual unity but the domination of the many by the "master race" on the basis of the superiority of the values of the conquering national state to universal human values. The price of defeat by a nationalistic state is not only loss of

[2] *The Spirit of World Politics* (New York: The Macmillan Company, 1932), p. 501.

political liberty and economic freedom but also loss of cultural autonomy and membership in humanity.

The development of scientific knowledge and its application in the form of technology and control of human behavior have provided the means both for complete regimentation of a people and the means for achieving world domination by a great power as well. The fact that Germany came so near to achieving its goal is a threat which destruction of German power, even if permanent, does not remove. For it is exceedingly naïve to suppose that the impulse to world domination is destroyed with the destruction of the power of Germany and Japan. In a world equipped with science, the rivalry for power between nations is both accelerated, since it is a matter of life and death to the powerful nation to permit no rival to become stronger than itself, and more disastrous, since the rivalry for power defeats its very end, namely, the preservation of the nation.

Power and total war

Unless restrained, the struggle for power leads to war and modern warfare is total war. The atomic bomb carried a step further what the results of air-borne demolition and incendiary bombings showed: every citizen of a nation at war is exposed to all the hazards of the battlefield. Since one of the primary aims of modern warfare is to destroy the enemy's industrial capacity, war is waged behind the lines on the whole of enemy territory as well as on the field of battle between armies. The whole territory becomes a battlefield and the distinction between soldier and civilian is obsolete. Furthermore, total warfare necessitates the organization and mobilization of the whole nation. Agriculture, industry, transportation and credit must be mobilized as well as armies. Science has revolutionized warfare. Almost everything can be converted by the scientist into military supplies and the co-operation of practically everyone is needed for the conversion, as Professor Shotwell observed. The total mobilization necessary for modern war has its inevitable impact upon our institutions and the values they embody and safeguard. Professor E. S. Corwin writes:

> With the possible exception of the Civil War, the impact of World War II upon our institutions is the most massive force to which they have ever been subjected, and the shape which they will assume after they finally emerge from that unparalleled pressure is still to be determined. . . . Even wars fought for the most generous ends can still spell disaster for that complex set of values which our Constitution aims to uphold and promote. In World War I we sought no territorial or other gains for ourselves except some guarantee that the peace following it would be a lasting one. Nevertheless, it was following this war that so sober and conservative a thinker as former Chief Justice Evans Hughes raised the question whether, "in view of the precedents now established . . . constitutional government as heretofore maintained in this Republic would survive another great war even victoriously waged."[3]

Professor Shotwell points out that the impact of total war extends even to the future.

> Total war, which covers the whole of national life, not only economic but moral, intellectual and political as well, is even fought in the future as well as the present, through continuing dislocation in a world of credit.[4]

Total war, in short, means that no person and no segment of life in the warring nations is exempt from its impact. Further, total war cannot be limited and isolated; like a maelstrom it

[3] *The Constitution and World Organization* (Princeton, N. J.: Princeton University Press, 1944), Epilogue.
[4] *The Great Decision* (New York: The Macmillan Company, 1944), p. 11.

draws almost all the nations of the globe into itself. All the nations to which the warring nations have access feel its influence.
The involvement of the United States in World War II had its
economic and political impact on the nations of Central and
South America; Britain and Russia sent troops into Iran; Germany drew Hungary, Rumania and Bulgaria into the war.

Total war is not only global but uncontrollable; its effects
can be neither limited nor directed. The consequence is that the
means necessary for winning victory not only threaten the
total destruction of the enemy but also threaten the very aims
which the victory is intended to secure. In an era of applied
science, no life, no institution, no value is immune from the
impact of war. Thus the total character of modern war has added
a practical urgency to the moral condemnation of war. Since
war is no longer an instrument which can be directed and
controlled by governments, the use of war as an instrument of
policy is an act of irresponsibility both toward friend and foe.
It becomes the vital concern of all the people everywhere to
prevent the outbreak of aggressive war. The hope expressed in
the Atlantic Charter "to see established a peace which will
afford to all nations the means of dwelling in safety within their
own boundaries, and which will afford assurance that all the
men in all the lands may live out their lives in freedom from
fear" has become an urgent and immediate necessity. Warfare
between civilized nations has become nothing less than treason
to civilization itself.

Power and the powers

The threat which modern war is to civilization will not prevent nations from struggling for power. The interests of
nations will continue to conflict. Thus the question of first
importance for this generation is to find an effective means for

curbing the power rivalries of nations, especially of great nations, and to develop a spiritual basis for world order. The dilemma which confronts us is that only the great nations have sufficient power to exercise an effective curb on the struggles for power, but the great nations themselves are involved in the power struggle. Recognition by the great nations that they themselves are involved in the struggle for power and therefore that their conceptions of freedom and justice are tainted with self-interest is a primary condition for escape from the dilemma. It is illusory to disregard either the fact of power or the inequality in the power of states; but it is a delusion—a delusion to which the powerful are prone—to believe that there are no limits to what power alone is able to accomplish. World order requires both the co-operation of the strong and the subjection of the strong as well as of the weak to universal law and justice. The doctrine of absolute sovereignty which has expressed the claim of the nation to be above any law except the dictates of its own interests is no longer tenable for people who esteem the democratic values. *"When Total War is the price of Total Sovereignty,"* Professor Corwin writes, "the price is too high." The question is, once more, not how nations may be rendered powerless, for that would condemn them to death; but how power may be disciplined so that it will be used for human ends and how force may be progressively subordinated to law. This requires a spiritual foundation, a political organization of peace-loving nations, and economic and humanitarian co-operation between the nations. It is a task beset with difficulties and obstacles, requiring good will, understanding and patient work. But the alternative to world order—the development of the requisite spirit and institutions—is chaos.

3. ECONOMIC POWER AND
POLITICAL DEMOCRACY

The struggle for power between nations, for all its vital and inclusive significance, is not the only rivalry upon whose outcome depends the fate of man in the modern world. Just as there is rivalry for power among nations so there is rivalry for power within the nation. Groups having conflicting interests contend for political power: control of the governmental machinery in order to organize society to secure and promote their interests. Owners of property or management seek control of political power; organized labor seeks political power; organized farmers seek political power; and Negroes seek political power to secure their interests which the practical monopoly of power by white men denies them. Not only is political power sought but also economic power and social power. The struggles for economic power among businessmen and between labor and management are characteristic features of contemporary society.

Some indication of the significance of power rivalries within the nation is given if, from the variety of power rivalry, we focus attention on the conflict between political power and economic power and the rivalry for economic power within the United States. For both these rivalries have an immediate bearing on the life of the common man and on the outcome of these rivalries depend in no small measure both the material welfare of the people and the extent and kinds of freedom provided.

Power and democracy

Political democracy stands for a diffusion of political power. In Lincoln's definition, it is a government of the people, by the people, for the people. It rests upon the recognition of the political equality of all and operates through a government of limited powers periodically accountable to the people. Democracy is essentially pluralistic and its persistent problem is to prevent the monopolization of political power by any one partial interest. For when any group representing a special interest secures a monopoly of political power, the inevitable result is not only the use of the government to promote its own interests at the expense of the welfare of the whole community but also to destroy the means of effective criticism of its use of power. Democracy, for all its shortcomings, justifies itself because it provides a restraint on the self-interested groups within the nation; and the exercise of such restraint is a necessary condition for social justice. For example, in the United States political power has been used, though imperfectly, to exercise restraint on the concentration of economic power. The Homestead Act provided economic opportunity to many; antitrust legislation illustrates the use of political power to break up concentrations of economic power already effected; the National Labor Relations Act illustrates the use of political power to correct the inequality in the bargaining power of labor and management by guaranteeing to workers the right to bargain collectively through representatives of their own choosing. In spite of these uses of political power, however, Harold Laski has observed that "the disproportion in America between the actual economic control and the formal political power is almost fantastic."[5]

The disproportion between actual economic control and formal political power presents a fundamental issue for democ-

[5] *Democracy in Crisis* (Chapel Hill, N. C.: University of North Carolina Press, 1933). Quoted by R. S. Lynd in his Preface to Robert A. Brady, *Business as a System of Power* (New York: Columbia University Press, 1943), p. ix.

racy. The only way that political democracy can maintain itself is by extending democratic control to the economic sphere. The alternative to the democratization of economic life is the monolithic state operated by a dictatorship. The basic reason for this alternative is the mutual relation of political power and economic power. Without democracy in business, political democracy soon loses its substance and becomes impotent. Thus the conflict between political power and economic power is really the conflict between the people and those who, now having control over economic power, seek to gain control of political power as well. This issue has emerged as the consequence of the inherent logic of the technological development of industry under capitalistic organization.

4. POWER RIVALRIES: ECONOMIC

The twentieth century in America has seen the concentration of economic power and the concentration of control of economic power without commensurate responsibility. Both the fact of concentration of economic power and the irresponsible character of economic power are significant. Three developments in the concentration of economic power and its control deserve notice: the development of giant corporations, the development of cartels, and the development of trade associations.

Corporations

In spite of lip service to competition, recent development has been in the direction of a noncompetitive economy dominated at strategic points by a few large concerns. The facts for the period preceding World War II are fairly well known: three companies dominated 86 per cent of the automobile industry; two dominated the can output to the extent of 90 per cent; 95

per cent of the plate glass was produced by two companies; four companies produced 64 per cent of the iron ore. The National Resources Committee, using three criteria of size, found that the hundred largest corporations under each respective heading "employed 20.7 per cent of all the manpower engaged in manufacturing, contributed 24.7 per cent of all the value added in manufacturing activity" and "accounted for 32.4 per cent of the value of products reported by all manufacturing plants."[6] Berle and Means have found that the trend of development is in the direction of large corporations.[7] They found that the combined assets of the 200 largest corporations in 1930 amounted to nearly one-half of all corporate wealth in the United States; that the 200 largest corporations in the period 1909-1928 were increasing in wealth over 50 per cent faster than all corporations or over two and one-half times as fast as smaller corporations; that the proportion of all corporate income going to the 200 largest corporations increased from 33.4 per cent in 1920 to 43.2 per cent in 1929. Lewis Corey found that the 248 "biggest monopoly corporations got 40 per cent of all corporate net income in 1937" and that "56 giant corporations in 1941 held 75 per cent of all national defense orders."[8] The inescapable conclusion is that most major industries are dominated by the giant corporations. And the giant corporations are controlled by a few hundred men.

The significance of this concentration of economic power is that it puts the giant corporations in a position to enforce on smaller concerns such policies as "price leadership," "sharing

[6] National Resources Committee, *The Structure of the American Economy* (June, 1939), pt. I, p. 102.

[7] *The Modern Corporation and Private Property* (New York: The Macmillan Company, 1934), p. 35 *ff*. The figures are for nonfinancial corporations.

[8] *The Unfinished Task: Economic Reconstruction for Democracy* (New York: The Viking Press, 1942), p. 247 *f*.

the market," "price stabilization," "non-price competition," and the like. They are able to enforce policies which affect not only smaller concerns in their fields but also the consumer, whose supply of goods and the price he pays for them will be fixed by a small number of men who control the field. The concentration of economic power has reached the point where it can compete with the power of the state, and even attempt to dominate it.

Cartels

A further development in the concentration of economic power is the cartel. The cartel is a combination of manufacturers, producers or processors in a particular process or trade; the independent firms entering into the combination contract to regulate output or prices or to allocate markets or specialized processes among themselves. The combinations in many instances are international in character, and some agreements have contained clauses prescribing the conduct of members in such a matter as allocation of trade territory during and after a war between the states having jurisdiction over the cartel members.

Cartels threaten a decline of material well-being through limitation of production and maintenance of high prices, restriction of trade and frustration of co-operation between nations. A former assistant attorney general of the United States declared: "Totalitarianism represents simply the ultimate consummation of cartelism—the final, full expression of the reactionary forces stemming from special privilege."[9] While Americans appear to think of cartels as peculiarly European developments, the extent to which American corporations were involved in cartel agreements is indicated by the fact that the Department of Justice instituted forty-three antitrust cartel actions in the

[9] Wendell Berge, *Cartels: Challenge to a Free World* (Washington, D.C.: Public Affairs Press, 1944), p. 3.

period 1937-1944. Cartels have been able to enforce agreements restricting production, maintaining high prices (or even raising them), allocating markets and eliminating or restricting competition by corporations outside the agreement. Inspection shows that it is precisely the largest corporations which enter into these secret agreements.

The vast and irresponsive power of the cartels has been described by Mr. Wendell Berge in comprehensive terms. He writes of the agreements made by members of cartels:

> These agreements admit of no sovereignty other than their own, and serve no interests other than the short-sighted aims of monopoly. This has too often resulted in situations which have endangered our national security, injured our position in the world economy, and denied us opportunity for the fullest use of our resources and labor. Domestically, businessmen have had to yield to the dictates of large aggregates of power vested in international cartels. What and how much they might produce, and to whom and at what price they might sell, have been decided for them. If they did not yield they risked elimination.[10]

Trade associations

Comparable to the power of the cartel on the international scene is the power of the larger trade associations on the national. American business has proved fertile soil for their growth. These associations have grown into a network covering American business and "into the exercise of powers and influence which in many respects now reach far beyond those of all except the more advanced cartels abroad."[11] Such associations

[10] *Ibid.*, p. 209.

[11] Robert A. Brady, *Business as a System of Power* (New York: Columbia University Press, 1943), p. 191. The following discussion is based upon this excellent book.

fix prices, limit production, allocate to members a definite share in the available business, and discipline competitors who refuse to abide by the rules fixed by the association; they organize and direct efforts to secure grants from government to aid their plans and programs; they have developed and propagate an ideology of "trusteeship" which is aggressively hostile to the democratic ideals of equality and liberty; they reach out for political power to extend their control and further their interests; they use various means to seek to use school and church to further their ideology. Such a description is a composite; only the largest and best equipped associations can carry out all these purposes. However, the logic of the trade association network leads to a few powerful associations whose aim is the "synchronization" of the nation's industry or business, the "mobilization of the entire business community," and which, by virtue of their organization, are able to give effect to their aims.

As in the case of the giant corporation and the cartel, the trade association is a concentration of economic power exercised without accountability. It is noteworthy that, in the case of one of the largest and most powerful of the trade associations, control of the association is in the hands of those who control the giant corporations. The oligarchic control of the National Association of Manufacturers (which claimed in 1938 approximately 4,000 corporate members) was brought out in testimony before the La Follette Committee: "It would appear that about 207 companies, or approximately five per cent of the National Association of Manufacturers, are in a position to formulate the policies of the association."[12] Further, the method of choosing directors centralizes control even more. Mr. Brady concludes from his study of the association that the local, trade, state,

[12] Cf. La Follette Committee Reports, pt. 17, p. 7385-87.

regional, industry and national conferences are not means for democratic control by the membership but rather means for gaining information of sentiments and interests in order to manipulate them and implement policies originating at the top —and the inner circle at the top is composed of those who control the giant concerns.

Power and responsibility

The significance of contemporary concentrations of economic power is in the fact that the control of this power, vested in a few hundred men, is not responsible power. With the development of the corporation, ownership has been separated from control. The owner of stock bears no responsibility and has no control over either the physical property or the enterprise. The very dispersion of ownership (not to mention such devices as nonvoting shares), far from having the effect of democratizing economic power, contributes to concentration of control without accountability to ownership. The phenomenon is, tersely: dispersion of ownership and concentration of control. The stockholder exercises no influence either upon the selection of management or upon decisions of management. He has, as Mr. Peter Drucker put it, "abdicated" his responsibility; indeed, it is difficult to see how the small stockholder in a large corporation could, even if he wanted to, exercise responsibility.

The real power lies with management. It is management which determines the labor policy, the amount of production and the price policy. And the management of giant corporations, as has been indicated, is in a strategic position to determine these matters in its fields, and through trade associations, fix the policies for the nation's business. When the controllers of economic power themselves are powerful enough to compete with or even dominate the state power, what power can control them? And

when the controllers of economic power, who are not accountable for their rule, can successfully deny or capture control of
government, the inevitable consequence is the destruction of
democracy.

The struggle of labor

In the economic field, management is engaged in rivalry for
power with organized labor. This rivalry is, however, a limited
rivalry, for labor does not seek (in the great bulk of the labor
movement—A. F. of L., C.I.O., and railroad brotherhoods)
the liquidation of the rule of management and substitution of
the rule of labor. Mr. Murray, the president of the C.I.O., has
emphasized the common interest of labor and management in
production, and the Chamber of Commerce of the United
States and the C.I.O. and the A. F. of L. have found it possible
to agree on a common statement of principles. In short, the
great bulk of the American labor movement is not revolutionary.

Nevertheless, the rivalry for power between organized labor
and management is real even if limited. The union itself is a
power organization, called into being to match the power of
management. Labor's demands on wages, hours, working conditions, production rate, firing policies, union and closed shop
arrangements, and so on, enforced by its power of organization,
restrict the power of management. And as labor, as in the case
of the C.I.O., adopts broader social policies such as the
annual wage and wage-price relationship, the infringement on
the traditional managerial power becomes more marked. The
establishment of labor-management committees in industrial
plants during the war may be the first step in a permanent
participation by labor in certain aspects of management—
hitherto exclusively management's prerogative. In its struggle
for power, labor has increasingly come to recognize that govern-

ment is not neutral and seeks, like management, to organize its political strength to secure its aims.

That the relation between labor and management involves a rivalry of power becomes most evident in the threat of, or resort to, a strike by labor to enforce its demands, and the threat or resort to a shut down by management in extreme cases and the various forms of attack carried on by management against organized labor. For the power of labor to enforce its demands rests finally on its ability to deny effectively to management the operation of its plant. On the other hand, without access to the machines, labor is deprived of its means of livelihood. Thus labor cannot and will not surrender the right to strike without signing its death warrant. Also for the same reason any attempt to destroy or prevent independent labor organization is a basic threat to its interests and results in a life-and-death struggle. Once management has come to accept collective bargaining, the way is open to various means for adjusting conflicting interests by negotiation, conciliation and arbitration; and, while strikes may and do occur, they are not accompanied by the bitterness and violence on the part of both labor and management which were characteristic of strikes to gain the right of collective bargaining.

Collective bargaining between organized labor and corporation management is carried on between corporate entities. In some fields the bargaining already is, as in Britain, on an industry-wide basis. Thus, how industrial capacity and man power are used is determined not by individual but by corporate decisions. The Labor Committee of the Twentieth Century Fund, pointing out the crucial significance of collective bargaining, stresses "the fact that the basic decisions of our time are group decisions, corporate decisions, union decisions, farm bloc decisions and not the solitary decisions of individual sellers and individual buyers."[13] Both the necessity of technology and of social justice have eliminated a certain sort of individualism and encouraged a sort of collectivism which stems from the interdependence of modern life. Modern industry has both deprived man of his independence of others and granted him a new independence of nature.

That workers, organized into independent unions, have sufficient power to challenge the power of management is a necessary condition for securing some degree of social justice. This is the justification of unions. Nevertheless, it is evident that labor unions—no matter what degree of "industrial democracy" they are able to wring from a reluctant management— do not themselves provide the full answer to the demand for social justice. For in the first place, the power of labor is largely a "negative" power—power to prevent a too intolerable exploitation of the workers; and, in the second place, as the history of the labor movement itself shows, the protection of the interests of organized workers has led (as every new social organization leads) to new forms of social evil, as well as a greater degree of justice.

5. POWER RIVALRIES: PROPAGANDA

Control of public opinion

Besides political and economic power rivalries, there is the rivalry for the support and control of public opinion. The power of propaganda has been amply demonstrated in the modern world in spite of a widespread scientific temper. By various propaganda devices, e.g., simple reiteration, sales for products (some useless and some harmful) have been increased;

---

[13] "Trends in Collective Bargaining: A Summary of Recent Experience," *Information Service*, XXIV, 37 (November 10, 1945).

misstatements of facts have come to be widely accepted as true; illusory fears have been aroused, hostility and hatred directed against weak minorities, and even the will of a nation to resist aggression has been undermined. Now opinion is a powerful factor (though not all-powerful) since no social organization can maintain itself for long unless it is supported by the majority of its members. Naked force, if great enough, may be able to destroy the existing form of social organization and establish a new one; but unless the new form of social organization gets the support of public opinion, the new form will collapse either as a result of internal revolt or external pressure. Control of public opinion is initially important to the beneficiaries of any social organization, since the continuance of their enjoyment of the benefits they derive from the existing order is to a very great extent contingent on creating or maintaining a favorable public opinion. Consequently, control of the means for forming public opinion is both an expression of power and a means to power. This is the reason the power to control opinion tends to coalesce with economic or political power (especially the latter) and the reason freedom of access to the means for forming opinion is a condition for the effective working of democracy.

In contemporary civilization, who controls the means to influence public opinion is a vital matter since technical means make totalitarianism possible. Whenever any one interested group—a political party or an economic class, for instance—controls the means of influencing public opinion, there will be less persuasion and more "propaganda": selection and distortion of facts to suit the purpose, reiteration and glittering generalities. And when a party is able to seize political power, control the means of influencing public opinion (including schools and churches as well as newspapers and radio) and is prepared to exercise the police power of the state with ruthless efficiency to destroy opposition, the people are rendered helpless. At the same time, technological developments, such as the radio and the modern newspaper, make equal access to the means of influencing public opinion very difficult to achieve. For these developments obviously confer upon those who have access to their use a disproportionate power over those who are excluded from their use. Freedom of the press does not carry with it the capital to operate a press any more than the freedom of assembly includes the price of hiring a hall or freedom of speech the use of the facilities of a radio network.

Without free access to all the facts, freedom to communicate the facts and freedom to interpret the facts, political and social freedom is illusory because intellectual freedom has been denied. Without such freedom, a man's opinion is made; he is not persuaded but rather indoctrinated. The process of persuasion involves the weighing of conflicting views and access to the relevant facts; and the only way to provide for the conditions of persuasion being present is to insure the dispersion of control of the means of influencing opinion. Where governments control news agencies or censor news to suppress unfavorable facts or views, both international understanding and good will are endangered. Wherever and whenever the less powerful groups within the nation are denied the means of presenting their case and so persuading others of the rightness of their cause, they are perforce driven to the use of violence to secure their interests.

Fundamentally the same reasons for the dispersion of control of the means of influencing public opinion show the necessity for cultural pluralism if freedom in the various spheres of culture is to be maintained. In this age of nationalism, the dominant nationality has persecuted national minorities (with some exceptions, notably the U.S.S.R.). Where religion is important, the dominant religion has been intolerant of other religions or even of different forms of the same religion. Thus Protestants have persecuted those who differed from their own forms of Christianity; Roman Catholicism (which has never surrendered the principle of persecution) has persecuted Protestant Christians; and both Protestants and Roman Catholics have persecuted Jews (who have suffered both because of their religious and cultural difference). Likewise minority groups holding unpopular views or belonging to disliked nationalities or races have suffered various disabilities, legal, illegal and extralegal, at the hands of the majority. The problem which confronts a democracy is, not how to achieve cultural uniformity, but how to achieve justice for minorities without destroying unity.

Two rivals

Western civilization in the social ruin left as the aftermath of the war is the battleground for two rival social and political philosophies. (Both are more than social and political philosophies and programs; they have the character of social religions, since they claim to have answers not only to the immediate but also to the ultimate issues of human existence.) Liberal democracy with its emphasis on private ownership and control in the economic sphere (the position represented by the United States) competes with communism with its basic tenet of social ownership and control in the economic sphere and repudiation of the tenets and forms of liberal political democracy (the position represented by the U.S.S.R.). Obviously these are the two extremes; Britain seeks to combine democracy with socialism and France seems to be moving in the same direction. Thus various combinations are possible with varying degrees of political democracy and of socialism. In broad terms, however,

the present struggle is between capitalist democracy and communism.

While the United States is committed at present to capitalist
democracy, and in relation to Europe as a whole appears possessed of a stable social system, it is not unlikely that the internal necessities of a technological profit system on the one hand,
and the demand of the people for economic and social security
on the other will lead to a sharper division between those who
support a system of "free enterprise" and those who reject it.
What the future holds will largely depend (assuming a generation without major wars) on the extent to which our present
system is able to provide employment, utilize facilities for production and provide a sense of social meaning for the workers.
The problem faced by Western civilization—including the
United States—is whether a choice between freedom and bread
will be forced upon the people of Western civilization.

The present rivalry in the United States is between social
and political programs that differ in degree rather than in
kind. It is a rivalry between those who would reduce and keep
governmental participation in economic life to a minimum and
those who press for its extension. The proposal to establish and
the opposition to a Missouri Valley Authority is a case in point;
the proposal for governmental building and operation of low-
cost housing projects and opposition to it is another. This
rivalry for public opinion touches the life of every man. He
is the target of arguments, emotional appeals and various forms
of pressure. It also touches the life of organizations and institutions. Schools are subjected to various forms of pressures to
rally their support for, or at least eliminate opposition to, the
policies and programs of one of the rivals. The content of
textbooks is evaluated in the light of the rival policies; academic freedom is won and maintained only at a price. Clergy-

men are dined and propagandized to secure their support for rival programs.

Partly within and partly without the framework of this major rivalry there goes on the rivalry between the advocates of the extension of democracy beyond present achievements and the advocates of the *status quo*. The struggles for elimination of the poll tax, for fair employment practices, for equal educational opportunities for Negroes are instances of the struggle on the political level. Besides such struggles there are the struggles between the attackers and defenders of labor, the advocates and opponents of anti-Semitism, the attackers and advocates of co-operatives, the exponents of nationalism and the exponents of internationalism. The rivalry of conflicting interests for the support of public opinion is preferable to monopolization of the means to influence public opinion. For the rivalry is a condition of the citizen having some power of choice, even though a restricted choice, of alternatives.

Religious rivalry

The rivalry for the souls of men extends to the profoundest depths of human life—the rivalry between competing religions. One aspect of this rivalry is the rivalry of sects, especially the growing rivalry between Protestantism and Roman Catholicism in America. But by far the more important aspect is the rivalry between Christian faith and the social and political religions of our time (liberal democracy, communism and fascism). This rivalry is itself the consequence of the fact that wide and influential circles of modern men have ceased to take either Christian faith or imperatives seriously; and since no generation lives without a faith, other faiths have filled the vacuum. What distinguishes liberal democracy, communism and fascism from Christian faith is that the former have in common the outlook that man's life can be perfectly fulfilled within the framework of nature and history. They are unqualifiedly this-worldly, more or less explicitly denying the reality of anything beyond this world; they look forward to a utopia realizable upon earth. Still liberal democracy and communism, unlike fascism, have something in common with Christianity, despite their differences from Christianity—a fact which has led some to identify Christianity with democracy or democracy with Christianity and some to identify Christianity with communism.

In America, where Christianity has not been consciously rejected, any sharp statement of the rivalry will be an oversimplification. For the most part, the rivalry between the social religion of liberal democracy and Christianity is not between consciously hostile competitors; nor are the two without important points of agreement. Indeed, each has something to contribute to the other. For, while the resources of contemporary social and political religions are inadequate to deal with the ultimate human problems and issues of existence, it is also true that Christianity must purge itself of obscurantism and also provide some guidance for the solution of immediate social and political issues. The fundamental issue which divides them is the vital question of world view and life view: the affirmation or denial of the reality of an eternal realm beyond the temporal world.

This is the issue which is largely responsible for the rivalry of school and church in forming the spirit of young people. The controversy aroused by the movement for weekday religious education on school time has brought into the open certain aspects of the rivalry. The movement itself is a protest against an educational program which omits religious instruction; some of the opposition to it proceeds largely from the conviction of the adequacy and even superiority of the secular outlook. The very fact that educators are concerned to find an answer to the question, how to equip the student with an integrated philosophy of life, is indicative of their awareness of the moral and religious confusion of contemporary society. The fact that the question of the relation of the educational presuppositions of the school to religion can no longer be avoided is significant in that not only the Church but Christian faith as well is confronted by a rival for the soul of man. Whether the school will be hostile or neutral or friendly to Christian faith is an issue which can no longer be avoided. But it is an issue that cannot, in the long run, be settled by mechanical arrangements. The outcome of the rivalry will depend on whether Christianity can synthesize with its understanding of the ultimate issues of life a just appreciation of science and significant contributions to the achievement of an ever greater degree of social justice.

6. POWER RIVALRIES: THE PROBLEM AND THE CHALLENGE

Power and the individual

Modern man is caught in the conflicts of rivals for power. He is more powerful by virtue of the development of technics and by virtue of his participation in larger units of social organization (the modern state, for example) than his fathers. Yet the very enhancement of his ability to act has given rise to new evils. The development of a technical civilization which has made possible a vast increase in production of material goods has at the same time threatened the modern man's security, depersonalized human relationships and robbed him of social status and significance. The great achievement of the modern nation state has quickened cultural energies and at the same time produced an international anarchy which threatens the existₑ nce of civilization itself. The increase in power has made the necessity for social justice and social harmony more urgent and also rendered it more difficult of achievement. And the increase in material power, political power and economic power requires for its creative use a corresponding spiritual development.

Caught in the competitive struggle for power between social and political organizations, the individual becomes increasingly aware of the limitations a complex society imposes on his action. The alternatives between which he must choose are made for him by the very instrumentalities which have endowed him with power. A technical civilization has its own requirements and necessities with respect to the organization of industry, the position of management and the status of workers; a world of sovereign nations is not wholly plastic, waiting to be molded into an ideal world community. What is so evident on the larger social canvas is true for the individual in his more immediate concerns. He can choose which of rival parties he will support, but his choice is limited to the existent parties and even more restricted to those parties—unless one is content to cast a "protest" vote—which have a good chance of winning; he can choose his trade, but the conditions under which he carries on are set for him, if he works in a plant, by management and labor union; he can choose his newspaper, if he lives in a city which has more than one or can afford to order an out-of-town newspaper, but his choice is restricted to what is available to him. In many of the spheres which vitally affect him, the individual must choose between the existing rivals for power. In most cases a refusal to choose means his disenfranchisement.

The use of power

The fact of power is inescapable; and rivalry for power is the context in which man lives. To ignore the fact of power is futile;

to ignore the rivalry for power is to live in a world of illusion and sentimentality. The problem which must be dealt with is not, How can power be abolished? but, How can power be harnessed for constructive purposes? Not, How can power be made impotent? but, How can power be tamed? For powerlessness is not goodness but incapacity or inability to act. Impotence, whether of individuals, or societies or nations, is not spiritual achievement but spiritual frustration. Complete impotence is death.

Power as a means is neither good nor evil in itself. It is ethically neutral. It is necessary if any ends are to be achieved. On the other hand, when power is made an end in itself, the consequences are neither beneficent nor indifferent but disastrous for social well-being. While there is a great difference between power as a means and power as an end, the possession of power even by those who seek it as a means to some other end is dangerous. The transition from desire for power to achieve certain ends to desire for power for its own sake is all too easy. Lord Acton's generalization that all power corrupts and absolute power corrupts absolutely has ample support in the lives of men of power. The possession of power tempts men to pride and arrogance and a cruel self-righteousness. The love of power is so strong in man that the other purposes for which power is supposedly sought not infrequently become the rationalization rather than the reason for an indefinite expansion of power. Power has its own inner dialectic: it tends to indefinite expansion and to monopolized concentration.

Thus the problem of power is twofold: the harnessing of power to constructive and beneficent ends and the prevention of tyrannical usurpation and exercise of power. To harness power to constructive and beneficent ends is no easy achievement; it is far more difficult than the harnessing of the Tennessee or the

Dnieper to generate electricity. Yet the task is imperative. The power of the great nations will be used either for imperialist ambition or for world order; the technological power of the machine age will be used either for exploitation or for an economy of abundance; the power of opinion will be used either to promote tyranny in the realm of the spirit or to promote freedom. World order, social justice and freedom for development of the human spirit: these are aspirations and, more, imperatives to which power must be yoked if we are to avoid a suicidal struggle for power.

Yet it would be a naïve reading of human history to imagine that the problem of relating life harmoniously to life is assured if only power is yoked to worthy ends. For the evils of the exercise of power without accountability to the people are too evident. The responsible exercise of power involves both that it be used according to established rules and not arbitrarily and that those who exercise it must be accountable to the people for whom and over whom power is exercised. Democracy, in short, is a necessary condition for the taming of power. Political democracy does not insure good government; but, by preventing the monopolization of power in the hands of one or a few, it prevents the evils of slavery or serfdom for the many. An extension of democracy—control by the people—into the economic sphere is necessary in modern civilization to prevent the evils of economic exploitation of the many for the advantage of the few. A cultural diversity, rather than cultural uniformity, is the condition of the freedoms of the spirit: intellectual and religious freedom, without which humanity is mocked.

Rivalry for power for the sake of power is an element, and sometimes the chief element, in human history. That rivalry is rooted in the nature of man. The task of man as spirit is not flight from power but the use of power for the material and spiritual welfare of all men rather than for the exercise of power over men. If power is so exercised, it is justified. That some men and some governments exercise power with more responsibility than others is true; and the difference in degree of responsibility with which parents, educators, clergymen, managers and statesmen exercise their power is important. Yet the differences are relative, not absolute. Partly because of the limitations of human insight, understanding and imagination, and partly because of a strong love of power and the corruptions of pride, arrogance and self-righteousness which attend its possession, the exercise of power is never fully justified by its effects. Measured by the law of love, every holder of power is evil. But once again, the alternative is not an ascetic repudiation of power (which has the merit of recognizing the evils which accompany the exercise of worldly, i.e., political, economic and social power) for there are no fixed limits to the degree of justice achievable in history. The alternative is the understanding that the dimensions of nature and history cannot contain the human spirit—an understanding grounded in the faith that the kingdom of Christ, in which the destiny of men and nations is fulfilled, is real. It is the reality of the Eternal which saves the temporal from meaninglessness; and it is confidence in the reality of the Eternal which delivers from despair.

FURTHER READING

BERLE, A. A., and MEANS, G. C. *The Modern Corporation and Private Property*. New York: The Macmillan Company, 1934.

BRADY, ROBERT A. *Business as a System of Power*. New York: Columbia University Press, 1943.

NIEBUHR, REINHOLD. *The Children of Light and the Children of Darkness.* New York: Charles Scribner's Sons, 1944.

RUSSELL, BERTRAND. *Power: A New Social Analysis.* New York: W. W. Norton & Company, Inc., 1938.

SHOTWELL, JAMES T. *The Great Decision.* New York: The Macmillan Company, 1944.

4

RACISM AND COLOR CASTE

Buell G. Gallagher

1. Racism as pathological disintegration. 2. American racism: the caste of color. 3. Color and Christianity: the early church, the Syrian (Nestorian) church, the African and Egyptian churches, the Reformation and the New World, the boomerang of missions. 4. The power of caste: control by stereotype, the axioms of caste, caste and church life. 5. Color in the world scene: the rising revolt, the place of Russia, the challenge to the Christian.

MOST poisonous among contemporary forces confronting Christianity is racism, the practice of the dogma that there is special virtue in ancestry. Exceeded in immediate urgency only by the necessity of avoiding the appalling prospects of atomic warfare, and more explosive than any other social congeries, racism in its various forms not merely endangers the survival of Western civilization: it threatens essential Christian values with extinction.[1] It is amazing and tragic to see honest and earnest

[1] In this chapter, I may appear to some readers to reach positive conclusions without giving full supporting data. This is in part due to the fact that I am here forced to deal in summary fashion with a vast amount of material which cannot be given full discussion because of space limitations. I have attempted to deal somewhat more fully with these

churchmen in our day talking about racism as though it were a matter which could be dealt with at leisure. My purpose in this chapter is to make clear the pressing insistence of the Christian concern over racism, and to reveal the character of that concern.

1. RACISM AS PATHOLOGICAL DISINTEGRATION

The pathetic disease of prejudice has reached its provisional climax in the doctrines of Aryanism. Developed by the Nazis for purposes of political expediency, the notion of the master race was expanded in the exigencies of military alliance and global warfare to include persons of widely differing ethnic stock, and the Japanese became (for a brief moment in history) the "Yellow Aryans." But even before the doctrine had been pushed to that absurdity, *Mein Kampf* had made clear Hitler's contention that "race" is more a matter of "spirit" than of biology. In order to include the diminutive dwarf, Goebbels, the brunet Hitler and the rotund Goering in the "race" of tall, blond Nordics, it was necessary for the party leaders to redefine "race" as a matter neither of biology nor anthropometrics but of *geist*.

The sinister purpose underlying this elaboration of theory perfectly illustrates the intrinsic meaning of "race" not as a biological datum but as a symbol and tool of conflict. Defining the Aryans as one "race" and the Jews as another and altogether different "race," the Nazis were able to set the two artificially separated groups over against each other, thus discovering a

same matters, giving supporting data and qualifying considerations, in *Color and Conscience: The Irrepressible Conflict* (Harper & Brothers, 1946) to which readers are referred for substantiation of the conclusions stated in this chapter. I wish also to thank the publishers for permission to use these materials in this chapter.

convenient scapegoat.[2] The Jews are in no sense biologically a "race." They are a heterogeneous and polyglot admixture of practically every racial strain known to mankind with the possible exceptions of the American Indian and the Australian Bushman. But by calling them a "race," the Nazis were enabled to set them over against another equally fictitious group, those who shared the Aryan "spirit"; and with the sheep thus neatly separated from the goats, to heap the sins of Europe upon the victimized group. That also made it possible to reach out beyond the geographical borders of Europe and to discover other "Aryans" who shared the spirit of the master race, and to include them in the world plunder bund. The fanatical fever of the pathological state thus induced made it possible for Hitlerian henchmen to shoot, starve, asphyxiate, burn and otherwise murder something around five million of the six million Jews who formerly lived in central Europe.

Back of this convenient mythology of Nazi dogma lies the work of Gobineau and Chamberlain, the one a renegade French Count who made up his racial theories out of his own fertile imagination with no attempt at scientific verification, and who confessed that his labor was prompted by a personal desire to vindicate his own family tree; the other an Englishman who exiled himself in Germany and became popular as "the Kaiser's anthropologist."[3] If we may rely on internal evidence in *Mein Kampf*, Chamberlain's work is the only book Hitler ever read. But neither Gobineau nor Chamberlain ever put a finger down

[2] Cf. *The A, B, C of Scapegoating* (Chicago: Central Y.M.C.A., 1943).

[3] Count Arthur De Gobineau, *The Moral and Intellectual Diversity of the Races*, tr. by H. Hotz (Philadelphia: J. B. Lippincott Company, 1856); *The Inequality of the Human Races*, tr. by Adrian Collins (London: William Heinemann, Ltd., 1915); Houston Stewart Chamberlain, *Foundations of the Nineteenth Century* (New York: Dodd, Mead & Company, Inc., 1912).

on a particular physical type or anthropometrically identifiable species of mankind and said, "This is an Aryan." They could not point to a nation and say, "These are Aryan people." The Aryan (or Teuton) was a mythical person who shared a mystical experience with others in a mythical world. The only definable evidence of Aryanism was the badge of the "Aryan Spirit." The utter meaninglessness of this nonsense is exposed in the statement of it; but like many another piece of knavery, when dressed up in sufficient verbiage and obscured by reams of jargon, it gained credence even among its victims.

Chamberlain's method of "discovering" and identifying an "Aryan" was to use intuition. He called it "spiritual divination"; and his method (if it may be dignified by that name) he called "rational anthropology." Using the terms Teuton and Aryan interchangeably, Chamberlain declared that the spirit of a man made him one of the elect "race." Many falsehoods have been spun into the fabric of contemporary racism, but none is less tenable than this one which is nothing but arbitrary definition of a mythical spirit, in accordance with which definition the non-Aryan becomes the legitimate scapegoat. If it were not clear that this mystical conception of a "spiritual race" has played a major part in history's greatest war, it would be impossible to believe that sane men could accept the myth. It may be, indeed, that sane persons cannot.

The point in beginning our discussion of the significance of "race" with this statement about Aryan nonsense lies in the fact that Nazism illustrates the lengths to which racism can go, and at the same time reveals the actual meaning of racial doctrines. Devoid of scientifically verified or verifiable support, racism invents a synthetic pseudo science and conjures up a mythology, relying on intuition and spiritual divination. It is witchcraft. It concocts its own "science" and burns the books of all others.

It uses "race" not to refer to any inherited biological realities, but to identify the conspirators as superior men. But for all its irrationality, it is a potent tool of culture conflict: therein lies its significance as well as its strength.

The bearing of the Nazi use of "race" upon the use of the term in America is not far to seek. Some persons among us hold it in precisely the same form as did the Nazis, and would apply it in much the same way if they had power. A much larger group, while attaching the term to an identifiable racial group (Negro or Oriental or some other), actually uses "race" primarily as a tool of culture conflict rather than as a description of the several species of a single genus, Homo sapiens. Thus the term "race" is given a specious genuineness in American life by being coupled with observable differences in skin color or hair texture or other physical features, or by being attached to ancestry; but that does not alter the fact that its principal function is to serve the conflict rather than to describe men.

I am not saying that there is "no difference" between men who are classified as Caucasians and men who are classified as Negroes in the United States of America. That difference, how-ever, is not as absolute as is frequently assumed: more than 70 per cent of the Negro caste in America today has some Cau-casian ancestry. Moreover, the primary significance of race in the American scene does not grow out of these differences in pigmentation and physique: it is expressed in the use of the concept of race differences as a means of supporting and elab-orating a caste system. It is to that system and its peculiar usages that we now turn our attention.

2. AMERICAN RACISM:
THE CASTE OF COLOR

There is, of course, no single cause of racial prejudice, no single explanation of the perpetuation of the caste system. A number of factors—economic interest, social prestige, prevailing stereotypes, sexual exploitation, compensation for poverty in the white caste, to mention only a few—work cumulatively on one another to keep the caste system going. The color line is both the symbol of the conflict and the means whereby it is carried on. As the crusader used the cross as a two-handed sword with which he fought and, at evening, thrusting its point in the ground to kneel in veneration before it, used it as an object of devotion, so caste serves the Caucasian both as a tool of control and as an object of intense loyalty. *In American parlance, "race" means caste.* The term is connected with surface differences which are being reduced in the passing of the generations; but this connection with color differentials only enhances the effectiveness of the caste controls. High visibility preserves caste status without the necessity of tattooing a caste mark on the forehead.

There is nothing mysterious about the manner in which these controls operate. They differ in intensity on the Negro-White axis as between the North and the South; on other axes, such as the Occidental-Oriental caste line, the differences in intensity are between the Pacific slope and the rest of the nation; other differences in degree follow similar regional patterns. But despite the difference of intensity, and with many minor nuances, the caste controls everywhere operate to keep the "color" line intact and to serve the exploitative and dominating purposes of the upper caste. The color line is thus merely the visible badge of the caste differential, and caste distinctions are a great gulf which divide the population into camps of antagonism. If, then, we wish to understand race conflict in America, it is far more important to understand conflict than to understand "race." When we see this, we are in a position to realize the full horror of man's most dangerous myth, the myth of racial superiority, and to see it for what it is—at best a lame excuse for an unethical caste system, and at worst a murderous lie.

There is no scientifically verified evidence to support the superstition that any racial group is, by virtue of its biological inheritance, innately superior or inferior to any other group.[4] Whatever differences in level of achievement (and there appear to be some) are now observable as between the norms or averages of diverse racial groups in America, can be understood in terms of differentials in opportunity, education and other environmental factors: such differences cannot now be charged to biological inheritance. For example, to give a Negro child a fifteen dollar education and expect him to do as well, on the average, as the white child of the same area who receives a fifty dollar education is cant. The differentials of caste, which work in favor of the white and against the darker man, are the causes of whatever "racial" differentials now appear to exist. Science has uncovered no racial differences in innate abilities; it has exposed disparities in achievement between castes. These caste disparities ought to be labeled as caste differentials, not as racial differences. But to do so would rob racism of its significance as a tool of caste dominance. Thus, in confusingly identifying caste and race, the American makes his own use of the myths of racism.

But the man who uses color as a tool of caste becomes the victim of his own operations. We do not need to minimize the price paid by the lower caste man in order to assert that the cost to the upper caste is also onerous. The psychological cost is incalculable: who will weigh the perversion of mind and spirit which result from the warping of vision, the dulling of understanding, the bifurcation of the inner man to correspond

---

[4] The reader is reminded of note 1, and encouraged to bear my apology in mind without further notation in this chapter.

to his schizoid society? The economic costs are more readily measurable: the net effects of poverty, disease and discouragement, in terms of low purchasing power, inefficient productive effort and the general slowing down of economic processes, are concomitants of caste. The cultural costs are equally significant: the impoverishment of American life through the rejection or the diverting of the ebullient creative effort of our minorities is high-lighted in the contrasting achievement by men of these same minorities in other parts of the world where the caste differential does not hold them back. And the spiritual costs of caste, which ought to be most apparent to American Christians, are the greatest of all: the fact that it is necessary to point them out is a demonstration of the bluntness of conscience and blindness of spirit which caste has induced among us. The division of the family of God in accordance with arbitrary[5] lines of color is a flat denial of the meaning of brotherhood. Such a denial can mean but one thing. As with Cain of old, he who denies the obligations of brotherhood, goes out from the presence of the Lord.

Nevertheless, expensive as it is in all these respects, color caste continues to hold us in its power. Like the old man of the legend, it sits astride our shoulders, winds its legs more tightly about our throats, and refuses to be dislodged. Where, in our journeying, did we make the fateful blunder of taking this lecherous burden upon us?

3. COLOR AND CHRISTIANITY

History is gracious: she conceals what men wish to forget. But when men wish to remember, she can stab conscience awake with the rapier of fact. Let us read the record.

[5] I say "arbitrary" advisedly, for that is what the caste line is. It corresponds to no intrinsically significant reality.

Christians of this century too easily glide on the trapeze of historical ignorance from the New Testament to the present moment. To understand the predicament in which we now stand, we must look at the devious pathways by which we have come to this hour. Generally speaking, Christians agree that the faith was pure and undefiled in New Testament times, but that it lost its pristine purity at a specified historical period. Protestants are accustomed to date the corruption of religion at the Donation of Constantine or the edicts of Theodosius. Catholics point to the Reformation as the time when Christianity fell. But whatever general truth there may be in these points of view, in matters of race the story follows quite different lines.

There never has been a time when the Church was free of controversy between inclusiveness and exclusiveness: it is this continuing controversy which is the ethical nub of the problem of race today. Before his home town people, Jesus of Nazareth pointed out that they, the Israelites, were not the only chosen ones of God. For his pains, he was threatened with death by violence. Before him, the prophets had initiated the struggle of universalism for victory over particularism. New Testament times were bedeviled with the division between Jew and Gentile, between cultured and uncultured, between slave and freeman, between Greek and Barbarian. Some of the sharpest words of the Epistles are directed against the exclusiveness of this particularism. To understand the modern church in its perverse identification with the heresy of white supremacy, it is useful to trace the outlines of this warfare through the centuries.

The early church

There is no precise parallel in early Christian history to the present racial heresy which infects Christianity: the notion of race as we know it has been too recently injected into history.

The present controversy over racial allegiance of Christians cannot be "settled" merely by citing Biblical passages or earlier rulings of the Church. The words may be similar, but the controversies of earlier times had a different content,[6] behind which it is nevertheless possible to discern fairly consistent threads of meaning in the historical development.

In the Hellenistic world (excepting only the Jews and Christians in it), the important line of cleavage was between cultural groups. It was not race nor religion nor government nor politics nor geography which distinguished the "Greeks" from the "Barbarians." It was culture. Political forms and procedures ignored geography and ancestry, and religion walked in the train of cultural irredentism. The Greco-Roman or Hellenistic culture was the means of the spreading of the Empire, and the acceptance of that culture was the badge of membership in the Empire and its society. Greek in the East and Latin in the West, together with all that is implied in the use of these languages and the corresponding thought forms and artifacts, made up the culture complex which identified the Hellene as distinguished from the Barbarian.

In this world, the Jews made up an island of exception; and from the middle of the first century, Christians (either regarded as a variant form of Judaism, or, later, as a new religion) also began to speak of themselves as a "new race" or "new nation," using these terms interchangeably to mean the same thing. The Epistles do not use the word "race" in talking about what we today call "race." What Paul did—and it is far more significant than the mere denunciation of racial divisions and distinctions —was to attack the divisions that were tearing the Church, and to declare that none of these could legitimately divide Christians. There could be neither Hellene nor Hebrew, Barbarian,

[6] See, for example, I Pet. 2:9.

Scythian, slave or freeman. No one had the right to shut another out of the full fellowship of the Christian brotherhood because of any sort of difference.

Constantine saw the point of this. When he was converted more than two centuries later, he cast aside the Hellenistic distinction between citizen and foreigner for the entire Greco-Roman world. He abandoned the prevailing attitudes of *Romanites* toward Barbarians, thereby bringing them within the protection of the inclusive religion instead of shutting them outside the protection of the gods of the *polis* and the *civitas* as they formerly had been. He welcomed the Germanic tribes, giving these former Barbarians a status of moral and social equality within the Empire and the Church.

Theodosius I completed the work begun by Constantine. With his double policy of federation (*foederatio*) and biological assimilation which encouraged intermarriage of Hellenes and Barbarians, Theodosius carried out the obvious implications of his obligations as a Christian emperor. There could be no arbitrary divisions among Christians.

That these attitudes of universalism in the Empire did not always appeal to the non-Hellenistic peoples as a shining invitation to equality is another matter. The cruder, less developed Teutonic and Celtic peoples of central and northern Europe were flattered by the new universalism of the Empire, and tended to respond favorably to it. The more advanced peoples of Africa, Egypt and the Near East were not complimented in the same degree: they tended to resist the new doctrine, resenting the paternalism implicit in its use, preferring freedom and autonomy to the specious universalism of imperial control. As a result, the nationalistic struggles of these established peoples of Africa, Egypt and the Near East against the dominance of the Empire forced them to reject the church of the Empire as well: the new universalism was stillborn. To the people along the eastern and southern shores of the Mediterranean, the new universalism was a cloak of political imperialism and cultural dominance.

This confusion was inevitable, made so by the fundamental confusion of method in Constantine's mind and actions. He sought to use, according to his own statement, "the secret eye of thought" to achieve religious unity, while at the same time using military force to achieve political unity. Just how difficult it was for subject peoples to recognize the working of the "secret eye of thought" at the moment when they were being ground beneath the iron heel of empire, we shall shortly see. Nevertheless, the universalism of the faith was recognized even in this moment when it was denied in defection.

The Syriac (Nestorian) church

Even before the harsh imperialism of empire was glossed over with the inclusive sentiments of the "new race" Christianity, an important section of the Church had broken from the body of Christendom and gone its way. The oldest schismatical church of Christendom, the Syriac (Nestorian) church was baptized in the blood of its martyrs when Shapur II played the part of an eastern Diocletian. Its missionary outreach was flung from the Mediterranean to the Pacific and Indian Oceans. An important testimony to the effectiveness of its missionary zeal is the persistence to this day of the "St. Thomas" Christians of Malabar in India, whose numbers in the twentieth century exceeded half a million, even though the mother church had dwindled to some twenty thousand persons under a single patriarch in Kurdistan. The alternative persecution and tolerance of Islam, followed by the sledge-hammer onslaught of the Mongolian Empire, drove the Syriac church out of its native territory, reduced its numbers and left its missionary children bereft.

The particular heresy of the Nestorians was not primarily a creation of the Syriac church; but its acceptance, espousal and promotion in the East and in Persia was very largely a corollary of its rejection by the church of the Empire. What the church of the Empire declared to be heterodox was automatically guaranteed acceptance as orthodoxy by the Syriac church. Standing on the remote fringes of the Empire, it was the first to break away from the imperialism of a centralizing church, using the Nestorian controversy as the issue on which the break was made. By the thirteenth century the conveniences of historical forgetfulness had determined that the church at Rome (indeed, its very college of cardinals) was completely ignorant of the existence of a Nestorian church, and had never heard of its vast expansion throughout the Far East. The patriarch of the Nestorian church at that moment was a native of Han-balik (Peiping), with twenty-five metropolitans under his direction in Persia, Mesopotamia, Khorasan, Turkistan, India and China, with a total of some two hundred bishops, each with a separate see. In cutting itself off from the Nestorian church, the church of the Empire had lost contact with the greatest missionary outreach of Christianity previous to the nineteenth century—not excluding the Roman Catholic missions to the New World and the Far East. The loss of the Nestorian church from the fellowship of Christendom was the first serious break in the inclusive circle of Christian fellowship. Asia was lost: the defection had begun.

The African and Egyptian churches

It was from Africa (present day North Africa) that Tertullian spoke for the church of the martyrs, defying the Roman

Empire in words which were not idle boasts, but which were borne out by those who were sawed asunder and stopped the mouths of lions. The African church produced an apologist like Tertullian, an organizer like Cyprian and a theologian like Augustine. It once covered what is now Tripoli, Tunisia, Morocco and Libya. It was reported to have had five hundred and seventy-nine bishops presiding over as many separate dioceses, spreading the length of the southern shores of the Mediterranean from the Libyan Desert to the western promontory of the contient. But of that once powerful church, the only traces which remain today in the whole of that area are the crumbling ruins of ancient cathedrals, skeletal remains of once flourishing life. The whole of the African church, having made a magnificent stand against the Vandals, apostatized in a body to Islam in the seventh century.

Much the same thing happened in Egypt. There, the church had spread from the delta to the headwaters of the Nile, and fanned out in a missionary movement into Abyssinia. It boasted a long line of distinguished patriarchs, theologians and teachers; and by the seventh century it was the accepted religion of practically the entire population of Egypt. The power and vigor of the Egyptian church had been shown in repeated defiance of the church of the Empire with its seat in Constantinople. Yet, when Islam arose like a cloud out of the Arabian desert, it swept across Egypt and on to Africa, completely enveloping the once powerful Egyptian church, leaving only the sad fragments of Christianity to survive in the present-day Coptic Church. Just as the Africans stood against the Vandals, so the Egyptians stood against the Persians: but both Egyptians and Africans welcomed Islam. What lies back of this double tragedy, in the loss of the Egyptian and African churches from Christendom?

No single, simple explanation will suffice. History is essentially complex, and simplified analyses do violence to historical fact. Doubtless the less rigorous moral code of Islam induced the less saintly of the Christians to prefer the yoke of the Prophet to that of the Christ. Probably a more important element was the decline of the inner vitality of the Christian Church as it ceased to be the church of the martyrs and became the religious arm of the Empire. Certainly, also, Islam had a greater holding power than Christianity when once it gained a following; for its law of apostasy which inflicted the death penalty on renegades gave its perpetuation the double guarantees of faith and fear. But this would hardly stop Christians from maintaining a faith for which they had gladly suffered martyrdom under the pagan Empire. It is not fear alone, nor all of these things combined, which fully explains the ready conquest of Islam.

Perhaps more important was the appearance of Islam in its early years as a sort of Christian heresy rather than as a non-Christian religion. Its use of the Judaeo-Christian tradition gave it an initial acceptance with other Christians who might themselves be out of sympathy with the centers of orthodoxy. But after all due allowance has been made for the fellow-feeling of one heresy for another, and after all other factors have been taken into consideration, it remains true that the great growing power of Islam among the peoples of the Egyptian and African churches was found then, as it is now, in the fact that Islam has no race complex.

The religion which had identified itself with the imperial aspirations of the Caesars could not claim the allegiance of peoples subjected unwillingly to the Empire. Ready for a new government, they welcomed one which was also armed with an inclusive faith, although they rejected both the Persians and the Vandals who, while they offered a new yoke in place of that of the Empire, did not offer the same inclusive religious brotherhood. After the seventh century, in Egypt, the Coptic Church shrunk to a minuscule: in Africa, the entire church apostatized to Islam. The total elimination of the African church and the practical loss of the Egyptian church from Christendom can be charged squarely to the false identification of Christianity with the purposes of Empire.

It would be an assumption unwarranted by the facts to conclude that the church of the Empire either in the East or the West deliberately cut itself off from the Egyptian and African churches because of what we today call race prejudice. Indeed, in both cases, every effort was made to retain the Copts and the Berbers within the Church—and to keep them tractable. What we are justified in concluding is that the refusal of the church of the Empire to accord equality of status and consideration to the churches in colonial Egypt and Africa made these latter susceptible to a rival religion and imperium which offered inclusiveness in place of exclusiveness, equality instead of inequality.

With the loss of the Syriac, the Egyptian and the African churches, Christianity became, for the first time, a white man's religion. In subsequent centuries it spread throughout Europe, winning the nominal allegiance of the tribes and peoples there emerging from barbarism. Thus, the loss of the darker peoples from the Church, and the subsequent spread of Christianity exclusively among the northern European peoples, gave our religion its false and fatal identification with the white race.

We are not saying that the membership of the African and Egyptian churches was "negroid." The residents of Egypt and of North Africa were Caucasoid Africans, principally Berbers in North Africa, and an admixture of Semitic, Ahamic, Nubian and other peoples in Egypt. What we are saying is that all these "darker" peoples, had they continued within the Church, and had they been joined by the army of the faithful raised up in Asia by the Nestorians, would have made the complete identification of Christianity with white supremacy somewhat more difficult.

Moreover, we have here an interesting refutation of the sometimes repeated notion that "Christianity doesn't seem to flourish among the darker races." This is one of the most engaging forms of the white man's pride of race; but it is not borne out by a survey of historical fact. When the darker peoples were in the Church—up to the seventh century—they furnished at least their fair share of the principal teachers, thinkers, leaders and spiritual strength. Five of the greatest theologians of the third and fourth centuries were Egyptians and Africans. Clement, Origen, Cyprian, Arius, Athanasius. The Coptic Church was a strong missionary church, moving out beyond the valley of the Nile to establish the Abyssinian church which still survives. The expulsion of the darker races from recognized Christianity thirteen centuries ago does not prove that only white men make good Christians. On the contrary, it raises the question of whether white men can be good Christians.

Is it too much to suggest that the slave trade of the sixteenth to nineteenth centuries would not have been as easily possible if the Church had not long before that become a white man's possession, putting black men outside the pale of its protective brotherhood? Certainly, it would not have been possible to defend chattel slavery with the excuse that it afforded an opportunity to bring the heathen black man under the gracious civilizing influences of the Christian faith—to save his soul by buying his body, thereby profiting the master in this world and the slave in the next. The whole history of American life and manners might have been profoundly different. It is not unlikely that there might have been no "race problem": certainly not as we know it today, if fifteen centuries ago Christianity had not carried through its *rapprochement* with empire and begun to look down its nose at the "lesser" peoples. The Church gained an empire and lost humanity. The magnitude of that disaster has been softened by the passing of centuries; but the historical process which culminated in the modern heresy of white supremacy reached a provisional climax in the catastrophe of the seventh century. Its greater and more devastating effects were unfolded in subsequent centuries. In the matter of racial inclusiveness, the Church did not so much "fall" from an original inclusiveness as gradually lose a continuing battle against exclusiveness. Twelve centuries of identification of Christianity almost exclusively with Caucasian peoples have all but erased the memory of that earlier, more inclusive church; and thus has arisen in our day a United States Senator who dares to declare, "The white man is the custodian of the gospel of Jesus Christ!"[7]

The Reformation and the New World

Whatever attenuated tendencies toward inclusiveness might have lingered within the Catholic Church did not carry over into Protestantism. Arnold Toynbee has performed a valuable service in pointing out the manner in which the Protestant white man made use of the Old Testament doctrines of the chosen people and of God's blessing upon the conquest of Canaan, in opening up the New World. With a literal-minded simplicity, the Puritan fell upon the American Indian and smote him hip and thigh with the blessing of the Puritan God. There is no

[7] Senator Theodore Bilbo, addressing the Legislature of the State of Mississippi in 1944.

blacker entry in the entire history of white supremacy than the decimation of the American Indian by the Christian European. In the name of God and of religious liberty, Englishmen and Dutchmen fell upon the inhabitants of North America with an abandon which was uninhibited by religious scruples.

It is worth noting, however, that the treatment of the Indians in those English colonies which were Catholic was not greatly different from the treament in those which were Protestant. The identification of Christianity with whiteness was complete.

By contrast, the Spanish and Portuguese did not eliminate the populations of Central and South America. They merely reduced them to bondage. The story of conquest, exploitation, despoliation, wholesale brutality and robbery, which is the history of the conquistadors, finds its beginnings in the contests with the Moors in Spain. In that contest (as also in the Crusades) religious and racial patterns were welded into a single pattern. The Christian was lighter, the heathen darker. The magnificent splendor of the Incas and the Aztecs was fit plunder for men who felt no inhibitions in carrying out their mission of conquest and freebootery. If converted and baptized, the Andean non-whites of the New World might enjoy a subordinate position in the Church; but in it or out of it, the non-whites were considered to be a lesser breed, rightfully enjoying a lower status in the eyes of man and God.

By the time the Dutch and English began to build their colonial empires in the New World, the pattern was well established. Nor was there a non-white segment within Christianity to cry out against this false identification of religion and imperialism. The details of the story are so well known that I leave it with this comment: in the Americas, as in Africa and the Near and Far East, when Christianity has capitulated to white imperialism, it has gained an empire and lost humanity.

The boomerang of missions

In the nineteenth century, a new form of Christian imperialism developed. It was not always officially connected with or supported by governmental and commercial agencies. In fact, it frequently incurred the hostility both of government and trader. Here, at least, the inclusive genius of Christianity began to reassert itself, in tentative form, sometimes arrogantly, sometimes falteringly. American and European Christianity reached out to the south and the east and offered to the peoples of the world the good news of Christ. The "Great Century" of the world missionary movement saw an outpouring of lives and wealth so stupendous as to stagger the imagination. Thousands of the finest young men and women of Christendom went out to the far corners of the earth, carrying the Christian gospel and rendering Christian service. After all allowance is made for the cultural imperialism and arrogant paternalism implicit (and often explicit) in much of the missionary effort of the nineteenth century, and after the connection of missions with the economic and political imperialism of Europe and North America has been fully acknowledged, the story of missions remains one of the most heroic records of altruistic endeavor which history has yet witnessed. The vision of a triumphant Church, marching like an army with banners, bringing salvation to all the world, has stimulated the imaginations and awakened the sympathies (and opened the checkbooks) of men and women of the churches as nothing else has done since the Crusades. We have thrown out the missions boomerang.

When we threw it out, there was no indication that we expected it to come back; but we certainly intended it to go out. The generation which threw out the boomerang was sure of the superiority of its faith, and tended also to be sure of the superiority of Western culture, the righteousness of imperialism, and the divine destiny of the white man to rule the world. With the compelling assurance of its faith, the nineteenth century drew back the arm of its strength and hurled the beneficent boomerang of the missions effort across Asia, Africa and the islands of the Seven Seas, awakening a great expectation in the hearts and minds of those who accepted Christianity.

A boomerang comes back. Christians around the world began to look to the homelands of the missionary effort for leadership and light. Carrying a gospel of inclusive brotherhood, the missionary found his converts taking that gospel seriously. He had either to begin to practice what he preached, or stop preaching what he did not practice, or stand condemned as a hypocrite. He chose the first alternative, only to find that this embarrassed the people in the home churches. They sent him out to preach the Gospel: they now found that this demanded that they, at home, begin to practice it. This may not have been the deliberate intent of the missions venture; but intended or not, the inevitable logic of the position of the sincere missionary ultimately drives him to take a stand which is sympathetic to the aspirations among the people with whom he works and with whom he identifies himself. The cultivation of self-reliance, initiative and self-consciousness in a world of nation-states, together with the spread of education and the growth of numerical strength in the indigenous churches, has meant that, whether intended or not, the missionary effort has become a part of the anti-imperialist thrust of colonial peoples. The missions boomerang has come back to smite the imperialism of white nations, as well as to confound the churches.

No one familiar with what is going on in the mission fields today can repeat the lie that the white man is the custodian of the gospel of Jesus Christ. It is in the mission fields that Christianity today is making its greatest strides toward ecumenicity, receiving its most cogent ethical interpretations, most vividly exemplifying inclusive brotherhood. The real question now becomes: will the white man measure up to the challenge of the gospel he has proclaimed as a Christian? Or will the churches of America and Europe repeat, in the twentieth century, the default of the Church in the third to seventh centuries, leading to another great defection? The answer to this question is bound up with another: what possibility is there of breaking the hold of color caste upon the churches?

4. THE POWER OF CASTE

Our racial caste system has its historical roots in chattel slavery, but it thrusts its contemporary tentacles into every crevice and cranny of the social structure throughout the nation. Slavery, as ownership of chattel, is gone: as a caste system, it remains. Its purpose is to keep non-whites in a position which, in one way or another, is inferior or subordinate to whites. Its devices range from lynchings and mob violence at one extreme, through legal enactment and extralegal manipulations of courts and police, to custom and etiquette as instruments of caste control.

On this matrix of caste-and-class as elaborated in the American scene, every individual weaves the pattern of his own race attitudes. Unless he is able to devise some other loom (say that of the Christian ethic) to replace the ready-made patterns of society, the individual is unable to achieve an appreciable degree of emancipation from the attitudinal patterns which are typical of his caste and class. Generally speaking, the attitudes of whites, ranging from friendly paternalism to hatred and contempt, tend to recognize a caste status in which all whites are in one way or another superior to all Negroes, who in their turn must in no way be superior to any whites; while the reciprocal attitudes which Negroes must assume in order to survive in a caste-controlled society tend to recognize this subordinate status.

Social stance is not so much a matter of *where* as of *how* one stands. A white man can move from a former ground of antagonism to a new position of tolerance; but, if the new posture is still one of superiority, the fact that he stands on new ground does not alter the basic character of the relationship which is assumed. A Negro may climb from grinning subservience to quiet dignity; but, if he must continue to observe the caste line in his contacts with white persons, he continues to feel the bars of the prison confining him.

Control by stereotype

The attitudes of caste become generalized into stereotypes which are passed from person to person and group to group, in time actually coming to have an almost independent force and power of their own. Ideas then control action. These stereotypes operate principally by governing the belief and conduct of individuals, very few of whom form their own beliefs about race either on the basis of their own experience or by taking account of scientific knowledge. The individual merely takes over the attitudes and stereotypes which prevail in the society into which he is born. Race attitudes in contemporary America are formed not so much through contacts with other races as through contact with prevailing race attitudes. The individual learns to react to the symbols of race in terms of the patterns of caste, and dynamically in terms of the caste struggle. He does not ordinarily bring his beliefs under critical analysis. Here, as in so many spheres of life, the important thing to know is not so much what a man consciously and deliberately affirms, as what he unconsciously and uncritically takes for granted. The caste patterns into which men are born make it inevitable that the individual in most cases will learn to accept the color line in precisely the same fashion as he learns to accept the dietary habits and verbal accents of his parents and playmates. Through the acceptance of ready-made beliefs (stereotypes), the individual forms his racial attitudes.

Therefore, while it cannot rightly be said that race attitudes are "inborn," it cannot be denied that men are born into a society which gives them their race attitudes. The patterns of caste, and the attitudes and practices which go with these patterns, are carefully and fully described in the "Carnegie Study of the Negro in American Life."[8] A century ago, it was men of religion who first began to use caste as a description for the patterns of race relations. Caste is today commonly accepted by students of society as the best notion with which to summarize the character and the significance of race in American society. We have a pattern of color caste: the important thing in it is not color, but caste based on color.

A child born in American society does not have the option of living either in a casteless or in a caste-controlled world. He has only the option of growing up in the midst of color caste, accepting or rejecting it, in part or in whole, as his learning and experience lead him. If he rebels against caste or rejects it entirely, he is doomed to walk a lonely road, to meet with numerous petty persecutions, to lose friends and alienate people as he goes through life, constantly out of step with the procession of his peers. The weight of social inertia is all on the side of the continuance of color caste.

[8] See bibliography at the end of this chapter.

The axioms of caste

Perhaps the simplest way to summarize the actual operation of the system of color caste is to describe it in terms of axioms which are demonstrated in its patterns of action and in the attitudes and beliefs expressed in its functioning:

(1) Any white man is "better" than every non-white; therefore,

(2) All contacts between whites and non-whites must in some manner express this differential; and thus

(3) The etiquette of caste must always be observed; and consequently

(4) The white man's floor is the Negro's ceiling.

These are the axioms which undergird the cogent expression of a man like Senator Eastland who rose on the floor of the Senate in 1944 to say, "I have no prejudice in my heart; but the white race is a superior race and the Negro race is an inferior race, and the races must be kept separate by law." The operation of these axioms is seen in the whole elaborate system of taboos and polite observances which govern such things as eating together in public or private, using or not using polite terms of address, the wearing of uniforms or other badges of service by lower caste persons when in the intimate company of upper caste persons or families, and all the other safeguards of social distance. The devices of segregation and separation are commonly resorted to; and where these are not used, some form of etiquette or ritual observance is used to indicate the difference in status. In general, it may be said that, with variations and inconsistencies, both in intensity and in configuration, these axioms are applied in every section of the country. The caste system is an established part of American culture, with particularly clear legal and social definitions in the South, but with general characteristics of similarity in all parts of the nation.

Caste and church life

The caste of color controls church life in America just as realistically as it masters other aspects of institutional life. In all of American Protestantism, the churches which have more than one race represented in the ministry of a local congregation can be counted on the fingers of two hands. And the total number of congregations embracing more than one racial group in the membership of local congregations is considerably less than 3 per cent. Thus, for example, one of the more liberal denominations, the Congregationalists, with a total of six thousand churches, is able to report that less than three hundred of these churches include more than one race in membership, and only one has a ministry which includes more than one race. The only possible institutional rival of the Protestant church in America for the dubious honor of being most thoroughly Jim Crow in its practices is the less enlightened wing of trade unionism.

This legacy of exclusionist practices which now controls the thinking and practice of American churches illustrates the power of caste controls. The Church which is committed to the gospel of universal brotherhood is likewise governed by the practice of racial segregation. And while some strides have been made in bringing together diverse races into denominational organization on a more or less equal basis, almost no progress has as yet been reported in bringing the peoples of mankind together in the worship, fellowship and service of the ministry and membership of the local church.

5. COLOR IN THE WORLD SCENE

That the problems of color caste are not an academic matter, but rather are of immense practical and immediate concern, is readily seen when we look at the significance of color in the world scene. Acting and thinking as though he were a majority, the Caucasian is actually a minority group in the world's population. In a total of more than two billion people in the world, the Caucasian numbers only three-quarters of a billion. Outnumbered two to one in the present world population, and certain to be much more seriously outnumbered as population trends extend into the next half century, the Caucasian talks glibly of the problems of minorities, without realizing that he is the world's number one minority. He rates a position as the number one minority problem, both by the size of his group and by the adolescent irresponsibility of its performance in the world scene.

The Caucasian minority has a majority psychology. Either in ignorance of his minority world status, or in spite of it, the Caucasian feels that he owns the world and all the "lesser" peoples in it. He adduces concrete evidence to support his feeling. He has thrown the girdles of commerce and trade around the globe, planted outposts of financial and political empire (with necessary military backing) in its remotest quarters, and built the cultural outposts which, supported by power politics and a show of military strength, have given him a position of dominance from which he looks down upon the subjugated peoples in much the same manner as a feudal lord was accustomed to survey his vassals from the castle tower.

The rising revolt

But the rising tide of resentment and antagonism among the pigmented peoples can no longer be overlooked or laughed away. Not only within the minorities of the United States, but from all quarters of the globe, the insistent demand for freedom from white domination and white exploitation is becoming a fixed resolve of the darker races. The colored peoples of the world aspire to a position of freedom from white control and to acceptance in a position of equality. They will endure white domination as long as it is physically necessary to do so, and not one moment longer.

At the present time, with the possible exception of Japan, none of the non-white peoples has adopted a racial attitude which is as brittle and uncompromising as that of the whites. There is yet time to act. But that time is rapidly running out. If we wish to live on a basis of equality with the pigmented peoples of the world, that decision must be translated into immediate action. Tomorrow will be too late. For if we wait a few years before striking a position of equality of the races throughout the world, the continued arrogant attitudes of the dominant white promise to be the stimulant of a counter assertion of the non-white. Frustration breeds aggression: a few more years of white domination will make it impossible to satisfy the aspirations of the darker peoples with anything short of subjugation of the whites. If we emerge into that period, with the lines drawn between the white and non-white peoples of the world, and an increasing tension stored up behind the dams of prejudice, the opening of the flood gates or the breaking of the dams may plunge the world into that final orgy of bestiality, a race war on global lines.

The place of Russia

In any alignment of the peoples of the world along the racial spectrum, with the whites against the darker peoples, the most favorable attitude which the white nations might expect from the U.S.S.R. is neutrality. The manner in which the Asiatic nations are already looking to Russia for leadership does not strongly argue that the Soviet Union would refuse to participate in such a conflict—on the side of the pigmented peoples, and against the white supremacy which is totally rejected within the Soviet Union. The Office of Population Research of the League of Nations published in 1944 its estimates of the future population of Europe and of the Soviet Union which indicate that in the next quarter century the male population of effective military age in the Soviet Union will have increased from thirty million to over forty-three million, while the comparable figure for the rest of Europe is a net *loss* of five million. "The gain alone for the U.S.S.R. is larger than the 1940 manpower of Germany, the Soviet Union's closest rival in Europe."[9] No careful estimates of the probable increases in the populations of other parts of the world are now available, but it is certain that whites will, from now on, become a progressively smaller proportion of the total world population.[10] A two-to-one ratio today will, by 1970, become about three-to-one, with Russia failing to support the cause of Caucasian supremacy.

If the policies of white supremacy continue to force the darker races into a common bond of hatred toward the lighter, the issue will eventually be joined in a horrendous struggle for world dominance in which the first and second world wars will be mere curtain raisers. That war will begin where the last one left off—or considerably in advance of it, with the robot bomb, carrying atomic warheads and guided by radar and television, being only the beginning of the end. Quite apart from the possible outcomes of such a conflict, the stupidity of any policy

[9] Frank W. Notestein, *et al.*, *The Future Population of Europe and of the Soviet Union* (Princeton, N. J.: Princeton University Press, 1944).

[10] Cf. Gunnar Myrdal, *An American Dilemma* (New York: Harper & Brothers, 1944), p. 1017.

which is calculated to increase the probability of the joining of the race issue in global war is beyond debate.

The challenge to the Christian

In the business world, bankruptcy leads to foreclosure. The Christian religion has always maintained that precisely the same thing is true in the ethical realm, that ethical bankruptcy leads to the destruction and collapse of an immoral order. If this is not true, then the notion of a God of justice and of brotherhood is erroneous: the whole concept of a moral order must be discarded or radically altered. But if it is true, then man errs grievously in putting his faith in the continuance of a color caste in which the white caste is dominant.

The alternatives to color caste are at least six.[11] Among these the Christian conscience must choose, and choose now, before the time is completely run out and we have no alternative but suicide. There is but one possibility before us which meets the demands of the Christian conscience: race must cease to have any caste expression. Color can (and will) continue, as an interesting surface phenomenon of which one takes note much as he notices that a man is red-haired or blue-eyed. But to erect on this foundation of color a horrendous structure of caste is to deny the Christian faith and to foredoom the exponents of caste to that limbo of history which is reserved for men whose moral insights are so perverted that they chose the downward path at history's critical moments.

With caste removed, it would become possible for Christians of differing color to be Christians: with color caste controlling us, it is impossible to be Christian. And if color caste continues for any appreciable time to control, the hazards not merely of survival for the white man, but of the salvaging of Christian

[11] See *Color and Conscience*, ch. VII and VIII.

values from the wreckage of global race conflict, confront us. Will it take such a conflict to bring Christendom to its knees before the God and Father of all mankind?

FURTHER READING

The entire series of the "Carnegie Study of the Negro in American Life." New York: Harper & Brothers, 1942-44:

HERSKOVITS, MELVILLE J. *Myth of the Negro Past.*

JOHNSON, CHARLES S. *Patterns of Negro Segregation.*

KLINEBERG, OTTO, ed. *Characteristics of the American Negro.*

MYRDAL, GUNNAR. *An American Dilemma: The Negro Problem and Modern Democracy*, 2 vols.

GALLAGHER, BUELL G. *Color and Conscience: The Irrepressible Conflict.* New York: Harper & Brothers, 1946.

————. *Portrait of a Pilgrim: The Search for the Christian Way in Race Relations.* New York: Friendship Press, 1946.

5

PERSONAL TENSIONS IN MODERN LIFE

Walter M. Horton

Introduction. 1. Basic types of personal trouble in modern life: fundamental conflicts, mental illness, maladjustment. 2. Basic factors producing personal tensions in modern life: interrelated causes, biological urges, family conditioning, cultural tensions, cultural disintegration and psychological tension. 3. Social consequences of personal ills: escapism, religious emotionalism, exclusive loyalties, war, guilt.

THE first three chapters have considered modern civilization from the outside looking in. The next chapter, if we may anticipate, views it from the inside looking out. From the outside its most obvious features are the pervasive influence of machinery and the power exerted by the huge racial, national and economic blocs; from the inside its most obvious feature is the disunity and uncertainty of the aims and standards by which its life is supposedly governed—"supposedly," we say, because our professed aims and standards would have to become more unified and less irresolute before they could actually govern the great unwieldly mechanisms and organizations we have inherited. From the outside, our civilization is as powerful and imposing as an advancing army of tanks plentifully supplied

105

with gasoline and ammunition; but *the drivers inside the tanks are obeying no common directive,* so it is hardly to be wondered at if the tanks collide.

It must already be evident that a civilization whose "material culture" and "spiritual culture" are thus dissociated and disorganized must impose severe and sometimes unbearable mental strains and moral conflicts upon the persons who have to live in it. Some of these strains and conflicts are suggested in the other chapters: alienation of man from nature, depersonalization of "people" into mere "masses," feverish competition between individuals and organizations for money and power, the solitariness and rootlessness of life in a world where all absolute standards have been dissolved by skepticism and relativism, the moral torture of choice between limited loyalties like those of race and nationality which make unlimited moral demands upon their adherents. In such a civilization, every person alert to the real implications of the situation must needs live in a state of mental and moral tension, the proper resolution of which may easily become the central problem of his existence.

The present chapter is concerned with the *psychological* problem of the modern person in the modern world: *how, in the face of such a dissociated, disintegrated, inwardly conflicting civilization, is it possible to maintain personal poise and mental health, so as to be a potential redeemer of this evil age, and not merely its victim?* Probing diagnosis of modern mental ills is our task in this chapter, for the first step toward a solution of this problem is to see its tragic depth.

Most of us know from experience that it is not easy for a person to keep sane and serene in the modern world. Modern life is a series of distractions and interruptions, a disjointed succession of disconnected episodes. (Turn the radio dial for proof!)

The family itself, the matrix within which stable character is formed and personality developed, is not a very stable structure at the present time. Is it surprising that domestic friction mars many homes, and divorce breaks up an increasing number, when we consider the lack of common ideas and ideals in our society? How can a young man and a young woman be expected to stick together for life, when they have no generally accepted "chief end" to which they give common allegiance, and no established code of conduct, which they feel bound to observe? And how can the children of broken homes be expected to maintain enduring marital relations in the next generation, when they have never felt the shelter of parental concord over their heads?

But even where loyal love exists within the home, it is likely to be invaded by the effects of chaos in the great roaring world outside, where storms are perpetually brewing that may strike hard upon the shelter of the home at any moment. Race prejudice intrudes, and a person honored among his kin finds himself the object of unforgettable contempt to those of another color or another ancestry. A depression hits, and the family is scattered by the necessity of eking out a living, while some members of the family are humiliated and mentally benumbed by prolonged unemployment. A war comes, and the family circle is disrupted by death, or by the destruction of the home, or by psychologically disastrous experiences.

The business of growing up and carving out a career is always tense and precarious, but in modern civilization, riddled with cultural conflicts, it is tense and precarious in special ways. Let us consider:

(1) *the basic types of personal trouble in modern life;*
(2) the *basic factors* that produce these difficulties; **and**
(3) the *social consequences* that flow from them.

1. BASIC TYPES OF PERSONAL TROUBLE
IN MODERN LIFE

Fundamental conflicts

There are three basic types of personal trouble, in every age. A man may be in conflict with himself, in conflict with his social environment, or in conflict with his Creator—expressed in a generalized attitude of fear or hostility or bafflement directed toward the whole Creation.

To the first type belong all kinds of physical diseases and the various sorts and degrees of mental ill-health, from mild indecisiveness and self-mistrust up through the neuroses (hysteria and the psychoneuroses) to the grand psychoses (schizophrenia, paranoia and manic-depressive insanity). Here also belong those types of character and personality which are self-contradictory, from slight hypocrisy and self-deceit up through alcoholism and drug addiction to Jekyll-and-Hyde duplicity, self-hatred and suicide.

To the second type belong crime and delinquency, which offend against the *legal* code, various forms of misbehavior which are contrary to the *moral* code, and "psychopathic personality" so-called, which violates the *social* code. (That is, if a man is to be received in a social group, he must not be a "bore" or a "crank" or a self-absorbed, self-assertive egotist, but show a reasonable amount of tact and consideration in his treatment of others.)[1]

To the third type, finally, belong all those attitudes of anxious mistrust or defiant cynicism or despairing withdrawal or persistent skepticism which make it impossible for a man to launch

[1] See L. G. Brown, *Social Pathology* (New York: McGraw-Hill Publishing Company, Inc., 1934), ch. XVIII, "Psychopathic Personality."

out upon the stream of life with any sure dependence upon the Lord of life or upon the inexorable laws and enduring values of life. The opposite of such attitudes is not undiscriminating optimism or pantheistic adoration of the universe, but a sense that amid much that is transitory and misleading and of little worth, there is an Enduring Reality to which a man may give his final trust and devotion.

From these basic types of human difficulty three intermediate types are derived. Intermediate between the first two types is what Dr. J. A. Hadfield[2] calls "moral disease." It resembles crime or immoral conduct in its outward manifestations; but it resembles a mental disease in its compulsive, involuntary, uncontrollable character. The kleptomaniac's stealing *looks* like ordinary shoplifting, but it *feels* like the suicidal impulses of a victim of mental depression, or the alcoholic's uncontrollable craving for drink. ("I'm going to town to get drunk, and Lord, how I dread it!") Intermediate between the second and third types is the case of the person who cannot be reconciled to God, or believe in God's reality, because he hates some human being, or has done wrong to some human being, and is unwilling to admit it. Intermediate between the third and first types— though often and regrettably confused with the type just described—is the painful and pathetic condition described by Dr. Georgia Harkness in her book, *The Dark Night of the Soul*:[3] "the sense of spiritual desolation, loneliness, frustration, and despair which grips the soul of one who having seen the vision of God and been lifted by it, finds the vision fade and the presence of God recede"—not primarily because he has sinned against God or man, but partly at least because some physical

[2] *Psychology and Morals* (New York: Longmans, Green and Company, 1936), ch. VI.

[3] (New York: Abingdon-Cokesbury Press, 1945.)

ailment, some glandular disturbance, some form of mental illness has clouded his religious vision and must be removed before he can feel "right with God" again.

All these types of trouble, as we have said, occur in every age. They are incidental to the process of growing up in a social and cosmic context which requires each individual to "integrate" his multitudinous desires in some coherent plan of life, and "adjust" them to the social and cosmic environment that supports or opposes them. It is neither unusual nor abnormal for the individual to experience severe mental tension as he adjusts his plan of life to the stark universal facts of life: birth and growth, life work and life mate, physical accident and social change, and finally death. Tension that disturbs a child's provisional integration of a few simple desires into a pattern of behavior may actually promote the integration of his character on a higher, more complex level. And trouble that jolts a man out of an attitude of passive conformity to his social environment may foster in him an attitude of "active adjustment" —an attitude that changes what is wrong in the environment, as well as in himself—which is psychologically sounder as well as socially more creative than his original "passive adjustment."

But there have always been forms of personal tension that are destructive, not creative; and in our time these destructive forms of tension have been too much for many people. Dr. Alexis Carrel pointed out in *Man the Unknown* that modern progress in the control of infectious diseases did not counterbalance the increase in degenerative diseases; and he concluded that the human physique was simply not built for modern urban life, and could not stand it. A similar observation might be made about mental diseases: psychiatry has made phenomenal headway recently in their diagnosis and treatment, but modern civilization seems to produce neurotics and psychotics faster than psychiatrists can treat them, even with the most improved techniques. Unhappiness, frustration and mental confusion are so widespread in the modern world that they constitute a kind of chronic, collective ailment, which makes people susceptible to acute mental breakdowns from time to time, much as a severe cold may make them susceptible to an attack of pneumonia. So characteristic of the modern age is mental illness (at least in this mild, widely diffused form) that we had better take a look at some of its principal varieties, before proceeding to discuss its main causative factors as clues to the chronic distress of modern life.

Mental illness

The most severe form of mental illness is what the law calls *insanity*, and medical science calls *psychosis*. Its symptoms are various, but they add up to such a general unwillingness or inability to face reality that the patient is practically living in a private world of his own. In *schizophrenia*, the most wide-spread form of psychosis, the patient's personality may eventually become so "shut-in," so insulated from every kind of external stimulus that nothing can stir him out of his apathy or bring a flicker of recognition to his expressionless face. In *paranoia*, the patient is not so completely cut off from the world. He reacts freely and sometimes violently to external stimulus; but his reactions are to a distorted picture of the situation, in which every item may be real, but its meaning is grotesquely misjudged because of some delusion that twists everything. In *manic-depressive psychosis*, there is no systematic warping of the world, intellectually, but emotionally the world looks, as we say, "rose-colored" in the elated phase of the disease, and deep, dark indigo blue in the depressed phase, so that at one moment the patient is embarrassingly ready to attempt the impossible, while at the opposite turn of the cycle the most trivial effort seems mountainously difficult to him.

Example A (schizophrenia). A girl in her late teens becomes uninterested in her school work, and falls asleep for hours at almost any time of day. Perplexed parents put her through a battery of mental tests, whereupon she makes several attempts at suicide and tries to run away. Becomes more and more confused and seclusive in her thinking, and is sent to mental hospital. Insulin shock treatment only temporarily restores her normal affectionate personality; she becomes increasingly inaccessible and strange to family and friends.

Example B (paranoia). An insurance salesman, Nicholas A——, after a rather unsuccessful career, begins to form exalted ideas of his mission to mankind. Takes strange interest in the place of *the Ass* in the Biblical history: the Ox and the Ass leaning over Christ's manger, etc. Has his picture taken riding on "a colt, the foal of an Ass." Associates this noble animal with his own name, "Nichol-ass!" Identifies himself with St. Nicholas (Santa Claus). Grows a messianic beard, and prints under his portrait, "I and the Father are one. I am for that I am the Sabbath." Writes letters to the President of the United States, the officers of the Mother Church (Christian Scientist) and the heads of the Roman Catholic hierarchy, demanding that they reform their policies and change their teachings.

Example C (manic-depressive). Mrs. X——, housewife, passes many years in a semi-incapacitated condition, owing to prolonged fits of melancholy. Sleeps late in morning, passes much time shut up in her room. Blames herself constantly. Listens eagerly to words of cheer, and brightens up momentarily, but soon feels as despondent as ever. Periodically, after rest cure in sanatorium, comes home bubbling over with energy, undertakes to clean her house, reform all her children's habits, entertain all her friends. After a series of social occasions in which she is the life of the party, and spends her energy lavishly, she relapses into gloom again, and does not emerge for another six months.

Maladjustment

Less incapacitating for social intercourse, less likely to require treatment in a mental hospital than any of the psychoses, are the common mental ailments known as *neuroses*. The most severe form of neurosis is *hysteria*, the major symptoms of which are *not* screaming and "throwing fits" (as popular speech implies) but various forms of "dissociation," whereby some one piece of mental equipment (such as the sight of an eye, the ability to digest food, a chain of memories, or even a whole set of habits and traits amounting to a personality) is so to speak "switched off," as though someone had pressed an electric button and cut off its connection with the rest of the patient's life. Amnesia, deafness, multiple personality, and what look like organic diseases of many sorts, may all be symptoms of hysteria. Less crippling than hysteria are the *psychoneuroses*, the main symptoms of which are feelings of inferiority and inadequacy, senseless fears and obsessions, and persistent fatigue, which tempt the patient to evade responsibility and postpone effort. Few individuals in modern life are free at all times from the milder forms of psychoneurosis, and great multitudes of people suffer from mental conflicts or slight "breakdowns" which would be diagnosed as hysterical or psychoneurotic if they became a bit worse. A great deal of *pre-neurotic* unhappiness and maladjustment in the lives of supposedly "normal" people is the fertile soil in which the psychoses and neuroses grow.

Example D (hysteria). A veteran of the Okinawa campaign has no recollection of the action in which he was wounded by the explosion of a *kamikaze*. Declines to talk about his war experiences at all. The sound of an airplane makes him start violently; he can hear a plane miles away, when it is quite inaudible to a civilian.

Example E (psychoneurosis). A dejected man confesses to his pastor that he has just tried to commit suicide—and failed at that, as he has failed at everything else he has ever tried to do. The pastor knows that as a matter of fact this man is regarded as very competent in his profession, and a very likable person; yet his whole manner constantly indicates that he mistrusts himself.

Example F (pre-neurotic conflicts). Mrs. Y—— protests that she is being overworked in the church; she wishes other people would show more sense of responsibility and not push all the hard tasks on a few over-conscientious people like herself; but whenever it is proposed to relieve her of any specific job, her feelings are hurt and she becomes very angry.

2. BASIC FACTORS PRODUCING PERSONAL TENSIONS IN MODERN LIFE

Interrelated causes

Why is it that mental disease and closely related troubles, such as "moral disease," loss of religious faith, etc., have become so widespread in modern life? The science of psychiatry, in its attempt to diagnose the causes of such maladies, has gravitated steadily toward the view that many factors interact in all such cases: the biological constitution of the patient, the character traits he has developed, and the kind of cultural environment in which he has to live—all these factors blend in certain "unique experiences" which are the key to the understanding of the malady. Character traits are both effects and contributory causes of glandular disorders and other organic factors. They are also both symptoms and sources of bad social conditions. "Our culture is sick, mentally disordered, and in need of treatment. . . . Society, not merely the individual, is portrayed as the patient."[4] As an example of the interaction of culture and personality in mental ill-health, consider the following:

> High rates of schizophrenia were found in areas of social disorganization. In these areas, especially in the rooming-house districts, the prevalent pattern is one of indifference. Many rooming-house dwellers who are not insane vary only in degree from the paranoid schizophrenic in the matter of indifference. European peasants, living in American slums but cultured in a simple village environment, have few assets for meeting all the sordid disorganization of an American slum. Indifference seems to be their only way to avoid disorganization—indifference to communication. What seems to be a fortunate escape from social disorganization actually becomes mental ill-health, a form of personal and social disorganization.[5]

This does not mean that schizophrenia and other mental ills are peculiar to our type of culture, or wholly the product of modern conditions. An examination of the cases described above will disclose that the shocks and strains which precipitated these mental ills were in most instances such as might have been encountered in other times and places. The teen-age girl in Example A had helped take care of a member of the family dying of cancer. She was inexpressibly horrified to realize that life held such dreadful possibilities. In effect, she said,

[4] L. K. Frank, "Society as the Patient," *American Journal of Sociology* (1936), pp. 335-344.
[5] L. G. Brown, *op. cit.*, p. 283.

"Good-by, proud world, I'm going home," and she withdrew behind a wall of alienation and indifference and increasing apathy, so that life should never again get at her to hurt her. The paranoiac Messiah in Example B had been humiliated beyond endurance. To cap a long series of failures and frustrations, someone had called him a "silly ass." Thereupon his mind began to do what Omar Khayyam confessed he longed to do: shattered "the sorry scheme of things entire" and remolded it "to the heart's desire," so that the insulting taunt became a badge of honor, and he himself—poor beaten mortal—became a combination of Santa Claus, Jesus Christ and God Almighty. In one bound, he jumped from the depths of humiliation to the heights of divine power and glory, as anyone is likely to do who loses his self-respect too completely. The housewife in Example C had been brought up by a neurotic grandmother, who fussed over and spoiled the child, fearing she might die young as her mother had. So she learned early to pity and pamper herself, and never learned how to budget her limited strength so as to use it steadily and wisely. The veteran in Example D had been terrified by a very modern weapon, but gunpowder must have produced similar effects upon the armies against which it was first used. The dejected man in Example E had been whipped by his father until his spirit was broken—which is very much what happened to Martin Luther when he was a boy. Finally, Mrs. Y—— had been disappointed in her hope to have children of her own, and was pushing herself beyond her strength (or ability) in the conscious effort to make church work give her a feeling of significance that she missed in a childless home. Again, a pretty ancient and universal situation. The effect of the cultural environment is not so much to be seen in the creation of precipitating causes like these, as in the creation of a general atmosphere and pervasive attitude that make such precipitating causes more deadly than they otherwise would have been. In a world full of constant little distractions, where the healing rhythms and calming sights and sounds of nature have been obscured by urban cacophonies and conflicts, and where the thought of God has receded into the realm of obscure speculation, men fall victim to mental shocks and strains which they might have resisted in a healthier culture.

Biological urges

Pioneer psychiatrists did not notice these wide, general, pervasive factors in the production of mental illness. They were inclined at first to emphasize biological, organic factors, as their medical training would naturally lead them to do. Pierre Janet, perhaps the greatest modern pioneer in this field, developed a theory of mental disease based upon the cost of various actions in terms of the amount of physiological energy they use up. The mentally well-balanced individual is the one who knows how to balance his mental budget; he refrains from costly high-tension acts requiring initiative, decision, social responsibility and command, if such acts will exhaust his preserves of energy and throw him into a mental depression. The mentally ill person is a person who spends his energies recklessly and afterward falls into a depression, or who becomes so afraid of overdoing that he hardly dares to live at all.[6] Underlying this theory is the assumption of a fixed income of mental energy, based ultimately on physiological processes such

[6] Cf. the portrait Janet draws of certain "wise men" who manage to get along by systematically evading responsibility. *Principles of Psychotherapy* (New York: The Macmillan Company, 1924), p. 168. On his scheme of mental levels and theory of the mental budget, see my report of his lectures, "The Origin and Psychological Function of Religion," in the *American Journal of Psychology* (Jan., 1924), pp. 16-52.

as eating and sleeping, and varying sharply from person to person. Some cases of manic-depressive psychosis, such as Example C above, may be adequately explained on this assumption; but there are usually other factors.

Freud, while taking many an unacknowledged leaf from Janet's books, challenged this basic assumption at one important point: *the neurotic, instead of being a low-energy type unable to manage his limited income, may be (and very often is) a high-energy type consuming his very considerable mental income in internal friction, due to repression.* This one observation would be enough to establish Freud's fame as a mental discoverer. But he overlooked another important observation which would have stared him in the face if he had carefully examined Janet's ascending scale of mental tension-levels: *it is easier and more disastrous to repress the higher levels of our nature than to repress the lower, to deny the social conscience for the sake of biological impulse than impulse for the sake of conscience.* Psychologically, the consequences of anti-Puritanical repression are just what Freud described in the case of Puritanical repression; the unacceptable element is only temporarily eliminated by being bottled up, and presently "revenges itself" in all sorts of indirect tensions which it exerts on the whole personality. Socially, and in every other way, the inverted repression Freud's disciples have often encouraged ("let yourself go") is far worse than the kind he warned against (unwilling conformity to stuffy convention).[7]

Freud's immediate followers, Adler and Jung, continued to explain mental disease as the result of social convention inter-

[7] Freud himself in his later writings developed a distinction between the "super-ego" (the organ of the "reality principle") and the "Id" (the organ of the "pleasure-principle") which leaves ample room for an appreciation of the importance of duty and conscience. But the popular impression of his teachings is as stated above.

acting with biological urge (libido). Their improvements upon Freud's theory mainly consisted in widening the conception of libido to include other basic drives beside sex. For Freud, originally, *all* human wishes are basically sexual, and *all* mental disease are forms of sexual frustration. As early as the First World War, the clinical disproof of this theory was already overwhelming. Sexually well-adjusted people got very bad war neuroses ("shell shock," as it used to be called) under artillery fire in France. Obviously, other drives than the sex drive could be repressed and cause complexes.

Family conditioning

More recent studies of abnormal psychology, both of the psychoanalytic and of the more "objective" school, tend to move beyond the older psychoanalytic point of view, with its stress upon the social repression of biological urges. It is now generally recognized that *"repression may involve any motive,"*[8] biological *or acquired*; and the search for the causes of maladjustment tends to focus upon *early childhood conditioning in the family group.* But since the home (and a little later the school) have as one of their main functions to prepare the child to live in the wider cultural environment into which he is born, tensions in the cultural environment are constantly being transmitted through parents, teachers and older children to the growing child, who registers them in the first sensitive responses of his nascent self, and often develops mental tensions exactly corresponding to the cultural tensions thus transmitted.

One contemporary psychologist who lays considerable stress upon cultural factors in the production of personal tensions is Fritz Kunkel. He says:

[8] V. E. Fisher, *Introduction to Abnormal Psychology* (New York: The Macmillan Company, 1937), p. 134.

It is one of the difficult and unavoidable problems belonging to our present cultural development that every child experiences anxiety and fright at the onset of individuality. . . . Ego-discovery is synonymous with a tearing-loose—even worse—with being cut off from the original-WE. . . . In bourgeois circles the WE-collapse occurs earlier than among the peasants and the proletariats. Sensitive children are affected by it more strongly than robust children; yet the catastrophic consequences do not differ very greatly.[9]

In other words, there is something about modern civilization which sooner or later breaks up the harmony between the child and his social environment, and makes it degenerate into a cold, rigid egocentricity, confronting other egocentric selves (even those nearest and dearest) with self-assertive or self-defensive mistrust. This may be true even where each of these selves strives valiantly to be "unselfish" in the ethical sense of the word. Self-centered, calculating altruism is perhaps the most perfect expression of the disease we are describing.

Various types of egocentricity in parents or in social groups produce various types of egocentricity in children. "Hardness" in the educative process produces two types of "hard" egocentricity in children: the aggressive hardness of the little "Caesar" and the passive hardness of the "dullard." "Softness" or pampering in the educative process produces two types of "soft" egocentricity: the aggressive self-display of the little "star" and the clinging dependence of the "home-child." Alternations between hardness and softness, as between two different parents, two different moods of the same parent, or between an indulgent

[9] *Character Growth Education*, tr. by Barbara Keppel-Compton and Basil Druitt (Philadelphia: J. B. Lippincott Company, 1938). By the "original-WE" is meant the original unity of parent-child-home, which "collapses" when the child becomes a conscious individual.

home and the "hard, cold world" outside, produce more complicated patterns of egocentricity. The problems of the child brought up in the "patriarchal" home of a peasant, the "individualistic" home of a bourgeois, and the "class-struggle" home of a proletarian receive separate analysis. Still the general conclusion is that in *all* walks of life, modern civilization makes it hard for children to reach a mature level of devoted participation in the greater social whole.[10]

Cultural tensions

The precise way in which cultural tension generates personal tension and sometimes mental illness in the modern individual has been analyzed with particular care by Karen Horney in her significantly named book, *The Neurotic Personality of Our Time*.[11] She calls the neurotic "the stepchild of our culture," exposed only in a somewhat higher degree and reacting in specially accentuated patterns to the same stresses which bring a degree of frustration and tension to the normal children of our culture. Her analysis may be stated in three propositions:

(1) *Modern culture generates fear, hostility, sense of isolation, etc., in normal people.*

Modern culture is economically based on the principle of individual competition. Competitiveness and its potential hostilities between fellow-beings, fears, diminished

---

[10] *Ibid.*, ch. 9, 10, 28-30. Royce in his *Problem of Christianity* (New York: The Macmillan Company, 1913), sec. III, argued that the educative process by which the individual becomes morally self-conscious (social criticism) inevitably fastens upon him a "moral burden" involving tragic tension between his acknowledgment of the authority of the higher social good and his impulse to resist it. There is undoubtedly a universal fact toward egotism in human nature, but I have always felt that the educative process *as Royce describes it* is characteristic of a *particular social system*.

[11] (New York: W. W. Norton & Company, Inc., 1937), p. 290.

self-esteem, result psychologically in the individual feeling
that he is isolated. . . . Emotionally, isolation is hard for
anyone to endure. . . . Hence the individual—and I still
mean the normal individual—is in the dilemma of needing
a great deal of affection but finding difficulty in obtain-
ing it.[12]

(2) *In some sensitive children, the too early experience of
these disruptive influences generates basic anxiety, basic hostility, hopeless insecurity.*

In general, experience will lead a person in our culture,
provided his life is not too sheltered, to become more reserved toward people as he reaches maturity, to become
more cautious in trusting them.

When a child learns too early and too painfully that it is not
safe to trust people he acquires an attitude of "basic anxiety,"
which is "an insidiously increasing, all-pervading feeling of
being lonely and helpless in a hostile world."[13] Anxiety and
hostility are woven together in this feeling, forming a vicious
circle in which each generates the other; yet the person caught
in this circle may find his depressing feeling so unbearable that
he represses it, thus becoming unaware of the extent to which
this basic anxious enmity pervades his attitudes toward people
and toward life in general.

(3) *In the frantic attempt to get reassurance, some
basically anxious persons are led to protect themselves against
their threatening environment in fundamentally incompatible
ways, such as striving both to win affection and to compel
obedience. These are the full-fledged neurotics.*

There are in our culture four principal ways in which a
person tries to protect himself against the basic anxiety:

[12] *Ibid.*, pp. 284-87.
[13] *Ibid.*, p. 89.

affection, submissiveness, power, withdrawal. . . . "If you
love me, you will not hurt me." . . . "If I give in, I shall
not be hurt." . . . "If I have power, no one can hurt me."
. . . "If I withdraw, nothing can hurt me."[14]

Along any one of these lines, success is conceivably possible,
but it is characteristic of the neurotic that he is afraid to put
all his eggs in any one basket, and tries successively or simul-
taneously to do both of two incompatibles: to woo affection and
to withdraw into himself, to dominate and to submit, to inspire
fear and envy through power, prestige or possessions, and to
be loved without stint for himself alone.

We cannot follow Karen Horney into her description of the
endless tricks and dodges by which the neurotic conceals from
himself his own anxieties, hostilities and inconsistencies, attrib-
uting them projectively to others so that they appear to
threaten him from without instead of from within; but it is
important to note her concluding summary of the parallelism
between these internal tensions and the cultural tensions that
produced them. She points to three basic contradictions in our
culture: (1) "between competition and success on the one hand,
and brotherly love and humility on the other"; (2) "between
the stimulation of our needs (by advertising) and our factual
frustrations in satisfying them"; (3) "between the alleged
freedom of the individual and all his factual limitations."
And she concludes:

> Those contradictions embedded in our culture are pre-
> cisely the conflicts which the neurotic struggles to recon-
> cile: his tendencies toward aggressiveness and his tenden-
> cies toward yielding; his excessive demands and his fear
> of never getting anything; his striving toward self-aggran-
> dizement and his feeling of personal helplessness. While
> the normal person is able to cope with the difficulties

[14] *Ibid.*, pp. 96-99.

without damage to his personality, in the neurotic all the conflicts are intensified to a degree that makes any satisfactory solution impossible.[15]

While we may accept Karen Horney's general theory of a causative relation between cultural and personal tensions, and her specific account of the conditions under which such tensions result in a neurosis, we may question whether she has adequately explored the reasons why modern culture breeds neurotics. Competition, advertising and the quest for personal freedom are certainly characteristic of Western bourgeois democracy, and produce many acute tensions; but why does Fritz Kunkel find neuroses developing in "patriarchal" and "proletarian" families, and not only in "individualistic" families? The disease of our civilization lies deeper than the sore spots to which Miss Horney points.

Cultural disintegration and psychological tension

Perhaps she hints at a profounder diagnosis when she remarks that neurotic anxiety has a normal basis in what German philosophy calls the *Angst der Kreatur*[16]—compare Rudolf Otto's description of the "creature-feeling" in *The Idea of the Holy*. In the face of the constant, age-old limitations of human existence, marked by such persistent facts as death, illness, old age, accidents, political and social conflicts and overturns, every individual has normal grounds for rational fear and reverent awe when he sets himself over against the world's vast mystery and feels his actual smallness and weakness. In a healthy culture, however, the individual finds himself not alone and not lost when he gets into trouble or when he faces the cosmic mystery. A healthy culture has an outreaching, centrally deter-

[15] *Ibid.*, pp. 288-89.
[16] *Ibid.*, p. 90.

minitive faith which points beyond the individual, beyond the culture itself, to an Ultimate Being who is the source of all finite beings, and the Judge or Saviour of His creatures when they reject or accept His Will. When the Will of God is recognized as the final norm of human values and the chief end of man, the individual need never feel lost; God and his neighbor are his potential friends, if only he is reconciled to God's Will. Death and disaster may befall him, but even so no ultimate harm can happen to him; for when he faces inevitable tragedy his neighbor clasps his hand and commends him to God's eternal keeping.

To make such a description of a healthy culture is to recognize at once that our culture is diseased—diseased in its overall structure, not just in particular spots. Time was, in the Middle Ages, when our Western culture had more unity in faith and morals. The Roman Church, which was then the custodian of Western culture, became coercive in its method of maintaining that unity, and revolt necessarily followed. Protestantism and the Renaissance divided the West into cultural areas, *within* which there was still unity, but *between* which there was war. Science and technology healed the breach externally, by giving the West a set of common means, enormously efficient, for getting what it wanted; but internally, divisions went on multiplying. Finally the surviving sense of meaning and value in the West became too feeble and too divided to dominate the powerful mechanical instruments it had created to serve its forgotten purposes. The instruments went on a robot rampage, and their inventors don't know what to do about it, for they no longer know what they want or what is good. The condition which must be cured, if Western civilization is to become fit to live in, is: general absence of faith, confusion about the laws and ends of living, and insubordination of means to ends.

3. SOCIAL CONSEQUENCES OF
PERSONAL ILLS

Escapism

The starved and distorted personalities we have described form centers of social infection, and give rise to general pathological trends running through the whole structure of modern society. One of these is *escapism*, which corresponds to the schizophrenic individual's effort to retreat from the world.

The escapist streak in contemporary civilization is a broad, continuous band, shading from escapist drama and literature at one end to suicide at the other. The need for a temporary "moral holiday," as William James called it, is normal enough. No one can or should keep perpetually at high tension. A liking for detective stories, South Sea romance in the movies, or the sport pages in the newspapers, is nothing necessarily unwholesome. But the drive to "get away from it all" takes more reckless and urgent forms, often leading to vain regrets which in turn have to be cured by a new plunge into oblivion. Amusements of this kind are forms of dissipation, not genuine recreation. Recreation leaves the individual refreshed; dissipation leaves him with a headache and a hangover, and a restless feeling that he needs something more to set him up again— perhaps "a hair of the dog that bit him."[17]

Alcoholism is, of course, the perfect example of the dissipating, non-recreational form of escapism. Its fatal attraction must not be attributed mainly to the physiological effects

---

[17] Cf. the analysis of the roots of sensuality in Reinhold Niebuhr, *The Nature and Destiny of Man* (New York: Charles Scribner's Sons, 1941), vol. I. On the psychology of alcoholism, Charles R. Jackson's *Lost Weekend* (New York: Farrar & Rinehart, Inc., 1944), has recently furnished a vivid case history.

of a habit-forming drug, but rather to the contrast between the power and glory the alcoholic feels when in his cups, and the flat staleness he feels when he is sober. Who would be a poor slave when he can be transformed into a king by drinking a magic potion? Sexual license has much the same fascination. The ecstasy of sexual union is a momentary paradise toward which the restless, frustrated modern yearns as a thirsty traveler in the desert yearns for an oasis; but the circumstances under which it is sought and found by the sensualist rob it of its anticipated charms. The union of the sexes is repulsive and disappointing if not accompanied by genuine love;[18] the moment there is a spark of love generated in the most casual encounter, there is a bid for permanency; but this bid is roughly rejected by the sensualist, and the affair breaks off with a cruel wrench that desecrates what love there is in it. Much the same alternation of high expectations and sinking disillusionments occurs in the case of the confirmed gambler. After a sufficient succession of alcoholic and sexual adventures, varied with experiments in gambling, suicide becomes almost a rational act. How much better to end it all than to go on with an endless series of self-deceptions, each awakening more bitter than the last!

Religious emotionalism

Closely connected with escapism is religious emotionalism. This is what Marx had in mind when he called religion "the opiate of the people." There are legitimate ways in which religion may bring comfort and surcease from pain; but the

---

[18] Cf. Lewis Mumford, *The Condition of Man* (New York: Harcourt, Brace and Company, Inc., 1944), p. 25: "Sexual play is the greatest of all forms of play; but when the person is reduced to a mere plaything, even the body feels degraded and cheated."

type of religion we have in mind brings the devotee a power and glory as temporary and evanescent as the alcoholic's. It takes him into a dreamworld of pleasurable excitement and then lets him down with a thud, uninspired to live any better than before, but anticipating the next protracted meeting as the alcoholic anticipates his next spree. It is a significant fact that protracted revival meetings of the type we have in mind are particularly popular in remote communities where there are no other recreational facilities to relieve the general drabness of existence. "O Lord, we don't want nothin' *ordinary* here tonight," prayed a woman in one of those meetings; "we want somethin' *extraordinary*." That expresses the function of religious hyperemotionalism in all of its pathos. It ministers to the need of relief from the meaningless round of the ordinary; but it does so according to the pattern of other dissipating, non-recreational forms of temporary distraction. In a certain isolated West Virginia town where protracted meetings had always been popular, the advent of the first radios and the first cheap movies put an end to the meetings by providing their psychological equivalent.

While escapism and religious emotionalism grow out of personal cravings, they have also their institutional, commercialized forms, which both supply and foster the cravings. The liquor traffic and commercialized vice are highly profitable trades; and it would be strange indeed if those who minister to the desires of alcoholics and those of sensualists did not do what they could to drum up trade. While many of the apostles of religious emotionalism are sincere men, there are some racketeers here also. (Lest we be misunderstood, be it said that religion without emotion is pale and unconvincing. But religious emotion should be a natural response to apprehended Truth, not empty "sound and fury.")

Exclusive loyalties

Another broad social trend growing out of psychological maladjustment is the tendency to give absolute loyalty to one's own race or nationality and to despise or hate all others. This tendency is at the root of the "new paganism" which in many parts of the world has replaced faith in one universal God with the ancient tribal cult of "blood and soil." Psychologically, it is intolerable to be as isolated and unloved in the wide, wide world as modern man feels himself to be. A loving God having ceased to be believable, the inevitable next step is to clutch at some substitute for God, something I may give myself to and by which I may be supported in return. The obvious next best to the lost Divine Kinsman is *my own kin*, whether defined in terms of race or class or nation-state. This deification of my own kin corresponds closely to the self-deification of the paranoiac—and springs from similar causes.

In the offering of this plausible alternative to God, neurotic leaders like Hitler have played a great part. That is very natural; psychotic need calls forth and supports a psychotic leader. The positive contribution of such leaders to the need of unity and orientation is very considerable; but unfortunately, when a limited loyalty is absolutized, it becomes necessary to hate and reject all outside the limited circle; and the resultant anti-Semitism, anti-Negroism, etc., finally destroys all positive values in the movement. Hate is made the chief basis of the loyalty that holds the limited group together; but unity based on hate is never so stable as unity based on positive values.

One interesting phenomenon in the sphere of group loyalties is the difficulty in getting quite such passionate devotion to any merely *economic* group as it is possible to get for racial and national groups. This is probably because the economic order has become much more depersonalized and disintegrated than other parts of modern civilization. In the feudal system, men were bound to men in personal fealty; in modern industrialism, particularly in large-scale production, they are bound together only by the "cash nexus" of economic self-interest. This makes genuine *vocation*, genuine self-dedication to a form of labor tending to serve man and glorify God, increasingly difficult. The modern labor movement, while it rescues its members from a sense of lostness, does not remotely resemble the old trade guilds in their ability to make work a sacrament, and inspire standards of excellence. It can protect its members from the tyrannical power which wealth exercises against solitary workers; but it has not found a positive universally valid goal which is fit to kindle love and devotion, and on which a reunion of labor with other alienated fragments of society could eventually be based.

War

The final outcome of all the accumulated tensions of modern life, both personal and cultural, is *war*. Schizophrenic escape and paranoiac self-assertion both find expression in it.

> Under the stress of prolonged internal or external conflict, men have periodically reverted to extreme measures in order to create conditions favorable to a state of one-directional movement. Deep in the remoter layers of human consciousness, as every observant psychologist knows, there remains for this reason a dear love of war. For in the passion of one intense purpose all of the conflicts of a life can be swept away like clouds before the wind. . . . In war I am lifted to a higher plane, and I feel the heroic ecstasy that is the heritage of the brave. Even in mortal agony I breathe through the nostrils of the

eternal hero, and all perspectives are romance-tinted. Pain
can be laughed at and death is only an incident.[19]

The fundamental reason why war is psychologically so attrac-
tive is that "peace" is so unattractive—and so unpeaceful! So
far as a belligerent nation and its allies are concerned, there
is more real peace in wartime than in peacetime. More peace
between the nations in the alliance, more peace between labor
and management in the nation, more peace in each individual
mind, where every humble task is ordered and dignified by its
relation to the one all-dominating goal of winning the war. So
soon as "peace" is declared, war breaks out: bickering begins
between the allies over the peace terms, strikes paralyze industry and a sense of confusion and futility creeps into each individual mind.

Not yet, but eventually, the subconscious conviction spreads
through our unhappy culture that what we really need to cure
this miserable hangover is "a hair of the dog that bit us"—
another "wee drap" of war to give us another glorious experience of temporary peace! Yet there is no truly satisfying peace
in war, either. Robert E. Lee once remarked during a battle,
"It is a good thing that war is so horrible, else we might love
it too much." For all participants in warfare—and in modern
"total war" everyone is a participant—there is a similar inex-
tricable mixture of attraction and repulsion, good and ill. The
soldier knows the joy of membership in his unit, which is part
of the united thrust of a great union of peoples; but he also
knows the shock and horror of treating some human beings
(the enemy) as he has been taught never to treat anyone.
The pacifist in Civilian Public Service camp feels at peace
with his conscience, to a degree, but vaguely disturbed at doing

[19] W. H. Sheldon, *Psychology and the Promethean Will* (New York:
Harper & Brothers, 1936), pp. 9, 10.

relatively insignificant tasks like chopping wood when he would like to throw his weight into something big—which public sentiment forbids him to do. The civilian buying bonds and carrying on necessary routine feels the strain of war, sometimes to a back-breaking degree, but none of its honor or glory. And back of all these specific distresses is a vague sense of woe at being a participant in something horrible—a sense of woe which *might* grow into a sense of guilt, but usually goes no further than general malaise. Unable to feel genuinely guilty, men are content with anxiety-feelings about themselves, and short-tempered censoriousness toward others.

Guilt

We have pronounced the forbidden word "guilt." This forbidden word points to the final conclusion of our diagnosis of modern personal tensions.

So far, our probing has gone down through three levels. (1) First, we considered the various surface symptoms of disorder in modern life and the various types of conflict and disease. (2) Next, we probed into the factors responsible for the prevalence of mental ill-health in modern life. We followed the lead of psychiatry as far as it would take us in analyzing our susceptibility; but we argued that a deeper cause was to be found in the lack of a central core of meaning and purpose in modern culture, the lack of any final reference to a Divine Will. (3) Finally, we noted the reflex effect of *personal* tensions and distortions throughout the length and breadth of our culture, generating racism, nationalism and war.

But with the raising of the question of guilt for these collective evils we reached a deeper level still. If guilt is real and not imaginery a diagnosis of human ills *exclusively* in terms of disease would be an incomplete diagnosis. Man is an animal with a conscience; and even when he is most mentally diseased, or most oblivious of moral issues, his conscience never wholly deserts him. The last chapter will take up the problem of moral conflict in modern life in more detail. But just at this point, before concluding our analysis of personal tensions and troubles, we wish to state our conviction that these distresses are not fully describable as diseases; they also constitute a state of sin, of which modern man knows himself to be guilty. It would take a depth psychologist, to be sure, to detect this knowledge of guilt; it is far beneath the surface, deeply repressed. Superficially, "modern man is not worrying about his sins," but he is certainly worried about something—worried nearly to death! And an analysis of his behavior shows him trying so feverishly to avoid looking God in the eye, that one is surely justified in suspecting that his worries have something to do with the fear of how he would look in God's sight if he should allow himself for a moment to see himself standing in that position! We have described escapism as a collective schizophrenia; may we now describe the evasion of God and the repression of guilt as the last and deepest of modern ills, resulting in a kind of collective *manic-depressive psychosis*. When God and conscience are repressed, only nature and mankind remain upon the scene; and throughout the history of the modern age they have fought an endless, inconclusive duel. When Nature's end of the seesaw is up and Man seems to be Nature's victim, man succumbs to romantic melancholy and despair. When Man's end is up, and he thinks for a moment to have become literally the master of Nature, he becomes as elated as a maniac—until the next blow falls, and humiliates him again. Advances in scientific knowledge can never cure these recurrent humiliations; we know that finally, now that atomic power is in our hands. The only cure for humiliation and frustration is humility and repentance—acknowledgment of guilt in the sight of God. This is a bitter pill for modern self-reliance to swallow; but when swallowed its bitterness turns sweet, and the cure of man's illness begins. For a world in which God's seat of moral judgment is once more firmly established is also a world in which there is again a "mercy seat" to which the disconsolate may go. In such a world there may be (and are) all the personal troubles we have described; but it may be said of all of them, "Earth has no sorrow that heaven cannot heal."

FURTHER READING

HARKNESS, GEORGIA. *The Dark Night of the Soul.* New York: Abingdon-Cokesbury Press, 1945.

HORNEY, KAREN. *The Neurotic Personality of Our Time.* New York: W. W. Norton & Company, Inc., 1937.

JUNG, C. G. *Modern Man in Search of a Soul.* New York: Harcourt Brace and Company, Inc., 1933.

MENNINGER, KARL A. *Man Against Himself.* New York: Harcourt Brace and Company, Inc., 1938.

SHELDON, W. H. *Psychology and the Promethean Will.* New York: Harper & Brothers, 1936.

6

THE SPIRIT OF OUR CULTURE

Amos N. Wilder

*The nature and importance of the "higher culture." 1. The
historical backgrounds of disintegration: medieval breakdown;
the outlook of the Renaissance; rationalistic and romantic
secularism. The influence of practical science and of science in
philosophy: technology, Freud, Darwin, Marx and Nietzsche.
2. The contemporary picture of cultural disintegration: relativism and anarchy in accepted values; the loss of ritual and community symbolism; rootlessness. 3. The beginnings of a new
integration: various aspects of the impulse toward community;
aesthetic and religious vitalities; the return to tradition.*

IT IS our task here to diagnose our time in its cultural aspects.
And yet the undertaking is a little more specific and a little
more difficult than that. For it is not our culture in its sociological features that we are concerned with. Other papers have
dealt with that. It is rather that which underlies the sociological
features and animates them, and which at the same time these
features bring forth: the values and assumptions and dogmas
that prevail. More than that it is the hurts and costs, the
gropings and tensions, all those more subtle and intimate conditions of life today where our culture comes home to persons in
their deeper experience. We are concerned with the spirit of

our culture. We have to describe, as it were, the weather, the spiritual weather, in which men today are born, live, wrestle and die. It is of this that any Christian understanding and enterprise must take account as well as of the more external factors.

It is true that when we say culture we tend to think first of all of those strata of society that are somewhat privileged or sophisticated. We think of those minorities that we associate with literature and the arts, with the colleges and universities, with the interchange of ideas and the sponsorship of philosophies and cults. But though movements of culture may advertise themselves most visibly in such circles, they are pervasive in the whole of society. They rise from general conditions, and all men in a given time live in this same all-enveloping weather, and breathe the same air and suffer from the same pervasive toxins and infections.

St. Paul had his way of distinguishing between the visible and the invisible aspects of that world against which he conducted his great campaign. There were, indeed, the immense structures of social and political institutions that stood immediately before him, blocking his path, the age-old citadels of paganism. In the trade guilds and the municipalities—whether the *colonia* or the free cities—in the sacred college of priests of Diana of the Ephesians or the civic pieties of Athens, in the massive power of Rome itself, he was confronted by the incarnate forms of ancient evil and his collision with these concrete institutions left him with many scars. But when he said that despite the open door there were "many adversaries," or when he said that at Ephesus he had fought, as it were, with wild beasts, he was thinking of the deeper foes, those spiritual forces that animated these visible institutions. He expressed it most clearly when he said that "our wrestling is not against flesh and blood, but against the principalities, against the powers, against the world rulers of this darkness, against the spiritual hosts of wickedness in the heavenly places." And he speaks again of these deeper fortresses and fastnesses of wrong and of the proper means of their overthrow:

> For though we walk in the flesh, we do not war according to the flesh (for the weapons of our warfare are not of the flesh, but mighty before God to the casting down of strongholds); casting down imaginations, and every high thing that is exalted against the knowledge of God, and bringing every thought into captivity to the obedience of Christ.

That is, Paul recognized essential foes in the spirit of Greco-Roman culture, in its dogmas and loyalties, its "imaginations" and its "thoughts" (*noēma*: "valuation"). To overthrow the outer citadels of blatant power he had to penetrate to the inmost keep where the evil was enthroned and where the visible tyrannies took their rise or received their sanction.

1. DISINTEGRATION: BASIC BACKGROUND

Our first task is to survey briefly the historical genesis and background of our situation. This story of what has happened to the modern world's faiths and assumptions, its traditions and loyalties, its order and its institutions, since the medieval period is not the whole story and is not as bad as it sounds. It bears upon the forms rather than upon the substance of Western society. The sum total of evil has probably not changed greatly, for the Middle Ages had their own way of brutalizing men and sabotaging the weal of successive generations, of condemning men and women before birth to attenuated and warped and blasted lives. And the very forces that have dissolved the older

patterns of faith and social structure have brought new liberations and alleviations. Nevertheless the modern story is in large
part a story of pride and of power, of new tyrannies for old,
new tyrannies of the spirit as well as of the market place and
the state. The particular constellations of evil today in our
greater theater require for their understanding this review of
the immediate past. It must be brief since our first concern is
with the present picture. And we must look primarily at the
cultural aspects of the story, leaving other aspects to those
studies in our common undertaking that are more concerned
with economics and politics.

It is particularly true of the cultural and spiritual life that it
can only be understood, diagnosed, interpreted in the long
view, in its organic relation to the past. Just as any criticism of
the arts is hopelessly lost if it isolates the present moment, so
with any assessment of the higher life generally. It is one of the
best signs of our time that we in this country are beginning to
see our day in a wider perspective. Today is not just today but
includes yesterday, and yesterday is not just yesterday but
includes a long past that is part of our conscious experience and
memory. The spotlight that we turn on ourselves has a wider
diameter. Thus our retrospect is not "history" so much as it is
self-analysis. The adventures and apostasies of our fathers and
forefathers are in our own blood and in a real sense are our
own adventures and apostasies.

Medieval breakdown

The cultural disintegration of our Western life had its
ambiguous rise at the end of the medieval period. The new or
renewed knowledge, the new and powerful social forms, the
explorations, brought about a growing revolt against the static
patterns of life and thought that had so long given a degree of

unity and order to the West. Spiritual and cultural authorities were undermined and the ruling symbols dethroned. This carried with it increasingly the dissolution of both religious traditions and religious institutions:

> The rebirth of a world forgotten and the birth of a new world. But also: criticism, undermining and finally dissolution and even destruction and progressive death of older beliefs, older conceptions, older tradition of truths that gave man certainty in knowledge and security in action. . . . A heap of treasures and a heap of ruins: such is the result of this fertile and confusing activity which demolished everything and could construct nothing or at least bring nothing to completion. Thus, deprived of his traditional norms of judgment and choice, man felt himself lost in a world grown uncertain. A world where nothing is sure. And where everything is possible.[1]

In the centuries that have since elapsed the process has continued. It has been rendered complex by the emergence of successive new but unstable patterns of order and loyalty. In these the traditions of the older world have reasserted themselves in combination with modern forces and movements such as nationalism and Marxism, or (in the more specifically cultural area) the Enlightenment and Romanticism.

The outlook of the Renaissance

The most fundamental feature of the Renaissance was that men passed from a finite into an infinite world. The medieval man's world had limits, whether as regards time and space or as regards the spiritual environment. This meant security, and therewith a kind of personal and social health. His demons were objectified, external and well under control. But modern man

[1] Alexandre Koyré, *Entretiens sur Descartes*, pp. 34, 35. Translation mine.

lives in an infinite world. The heavenly spaces terrify him. Science finds no limits whether it looks within or without, whether it looks backward or forward. Psychologically, modern man looks into himself and sees no bottom. He has "the sense of the abyss." He has moved from a world of Being into a world of Becoming. The change of outlook no doubt made for exhilaration but it also made for vertigo and even terror.

> What properties define our person since
> This massive vagueness moved in on our lives,
> What laws require our substance to exist?
> Our strands of private order are dissolved
> And lost our routes to self-inheritance,
> Position and Relation are dismissed,
> An epoch's Providence is quite worn out,
> The lion of Nothing chases us about.[2]

Erich Fromm has shown that freedom is an ambiguous gift. The opening up of infinite possibilities induces disquietude and a constant apprehension, since man misses the former limits and authorities. He is thrust into a period of lostness in which the new emancipations and powers are bought at the price of profound psychological tensions. Moreover, with new liberations come new possibilities of enslavement. Remove the religious or philosophical restraints on freedom of action, and men proceed to act in such ways as to deprive others of their freedom. The abuse of economic power was soon to illustrate this.

Secularism

It has often been pointed out that our modern outlook dates rather from the Enlightenment and the eighteenth century than

[2] W. H. Auden, "Christmas 1940," from *The Collected Poetry of W. H. Auden* (New York: Random House, Inc., 1945), p. 119. Quoted by permission.

from the Renaissance and the Reformation. A truly pervasive rationalism appears not with the first clear formulations of scientific method and empiricism in the sixteenth century, but two centuries later. Yet the secularization of Western society proceeded apace from the time of Bacon and Descartes. The new vitalities of the emerging nations of northern Europe with their new contacts and stimuli burst the bonds of authority. A new self-consciousness of the individual emerged, at once more assertive and more complex. The wider diffusion of influences, the new curiosities, the autonomy of the self, all collaborated with the rising rationalism to break up the hold of the classical and Biblical world pictures. In the difference between John Milton and John Donne, one can recognize the cleavage that was arising. Though Milton was strongly stamped with Renaissance humanism at many points and though his theology was daringly heretical, yet in his world picture and his use of symbolism he belongs to the old order. John Donne, on the other hand, in his sensitiveness to the new modes of consciousness, in his complexity and restlessness, is prophetic of our present outlook, and it is for this reason that he is so much cultivated by modern critics and writers. Men were coming out of the older securities and their nerves were exposed to experience both outer and inner in a way that made for fuller personal fulfillment but also for risks and anguish. Though the eighteenth century by and large voiced its rationalism in a framework of Christian faith, it had really cut loose from the older faith as measured by its essentials.

Then appeared the vitalistic impulse we know as Romanticism—a pagan upsurge from the deeper energies of the northern European peoples. In various subtle combinations with the attenuated Christianity of the age, it brought forth a host of literary and artistic creations and correspondingly a general culture characterized by sentiment and emotional exuberance, idealistic philosophies and revolutionary iconoclasm in politics and society. The middle classes of today still live in a world blessed and misled by the sentiments and valuations that were the legacy of that period. The religious ethos of middle-class life today bears the stamp of that experience. One of the first things that the Church of today has to do in its postwar penitence is to come out from under the spell cast upon it by Romanticism. One may say also that a similar repudiation is due on the part of many religious groups among us of the heritage of eighteenth-century rationalism. Granted that the larger part of our religious bodies need more rather than less rationalism, nevertheless its chilling, impoverishing influence on some religious groups and on wider cultural circles is as evident as is the fateful secularization consequent on Romanticism.

Science in practice

But other and more recent influences have affected our contemporary picture. Here it is not science or a world view but the outcomes of science in technology and the industrial revolution that demand attention. Randal Jarrell in "The Emancipators" addresses the pioneers of science and confronts them with the sorry picture of today, asking them if they forsaw what "Trade" would do with their equations and inventions:

> You guessed this? The earth's face altering with iron,
> The smoke ranged like a wall against the day?
> The equations metamorphose into use: the free
> Drag their slight bones from tenements to vote
> To die with their children in your factories.

> Man is born in chains, yet everywhere we see him dead.
> On your earth they sell nothing but our lives.

You knew that what you died for was our deaths?
You learned, those years, that all men wish is Trade?
It was you who understood, it is we who change.[3]

Setting aside the strictly social consequences of technology, no
one can exaggerate its effects upon the spirit of modern culture.
We shall deal with these in their contemporary manifestations
below. Empires of economic power have developed which have
affected not only the economic but also the spiritual experience of men. Inherited faiths have been dissolved by the new
social patterns even more effectively than by the march of scientism. If scientism has slain its thousands, a mercantile society
and an industrial society following it have slain their ten thousands! And out of the changing economic scene sprang a new
extension of science, the Marxian analysis of society with its
convincing exposure of the self-deception that characterizes
many of the ideals of men, the mask that veils the vast amoral
or immoral forces of social organization. This disclosure of the
realities of the common life furthered the discomfiture whether
of religious faith or of the liberal tradition and constitutes one
of the chief factors in contemporary negation. Insufficient awareness of all these matters constitutes one of the chief liabilities
of the middle-class churches today.

Science in philosophy

A corresponding breach in the vestiges of inherited securities was opened by the work of Freud and others. This too was
an extension of the field of science, only comparable in its significance with the work of Darwin and Marx. Here too a mask
was torn off the realities of life, in this case the life of the soul.
Men were made aware of the irrational factors in human con-

[3] Reprinted from *Little Friend, Little Friend* by Randal Jarrell, by
permission of The Dial Press, Inc. Copyright Dial.

duct. The powerful cables, carriers of the high voltage of our profounder impulses and drives, were disclosed at work in all their potencies over our conscious behavior, values and rationality. Thus science on its various fronts seemed not only to have discredited the scriptural and traditional basis of religion and the illusions as to its ideals, but also to have identified realities in human behavior that are beyond the control of either reason or faith. Add to this the effects of war as we have known it since 1914 and the social costs of the depression, and the wide prevalence of negation in the modern mood is understandable.

We may return to the figure of Neitzsche to find one who lived in the crosscurrents of our latter-day culture, and who illustrates points we have made and others we have had to pass over. He was also prophetic of what has since come to pass. He came from the petty *bourgeoisie* of a somewhat developed period of industrialism and philistinism, and protested against these. At the same time he was the product of a second wave of the Romantic movement, one which attached its creative enthusiasm particularly to the idea of a German culture. Of this too Nietzsche became critical. He is in one chief aspect the representative iconoclast and the father of modern secular protestants, come-outers and Bohemians. But his protests are significant: against all prosaic naturalism and the philistinism consequent on industrialization; against the mechanization and depersonalization of modern life; against barbarism and mediocrity, and this carried with it a rejection of democracy, socialism and Christianity, conceived as mass concepts intolerant of excellence and distinction; against all barren scholarship, historicism and metaphysics; and against the rising German nationalism. Nietzsche's appeal was to intuitional and instinctive authority. He opposed the hero to the saint. The solitude that he represented and confessed was not only that of the prophet but that of the self of our time whose roots are broken. He is the prototype of all the modern prophets who have fled the "bourgeois plain" because its atmosphere was too stifling and who have sought one or the other cult of salvation in irrationalism or mysticism to replace the God who was dead.

2. DISINTEGRATION: THE CONTEMPORARY PICTURE

The above retrospect has already suggested the chief features of our present disorder, but we have now to chart them more particularly and in their recent development as of today. The various resurgences toward new or renewed orders and faiths we defer to a third section. We continue to bear in mind that our special concern is with the spirit rather than the structure of our culture.

The anarchy of values

We note first the loss of absolutes in our world. The situation is variously described as one characterized by eclecticism, by a loss of criteria, as "a crises in valuations." As Thomas Mann's Joseph found out in Egypt: "the world has many centers." This relativity extends of course to morals. The historical review has shown the part of science in relativizing men's outlook. But it is not as though science itself, not to mention the separate sciences, spoke with a single voice. Says Max Planck: "We are living in a moment of crisis. In every branch of our spiritual and material civilization we seem to have arrived at a critical turning point . . . there is scarcely a scientific axiom that is not now-a-days denied by somebody."[4]

[4] Quoted by Harry Slochauer, *No Voice is Wholly Lost* (New York: Creative Age Press, 1945), p. vii.

Healthy societies require a certain degree of agreement if not in general ideas at least in basic assumptions. John Oldham in *The Christian News-Letter* (No. 174) goes so far as to urge "the need of fundamental conformity." He is not countenancing official dogma or coercion from above, but he is warning that an anarchy of ideas and values will bring with it ruinous social anarchy. History shows that creative communities and cultures have, each of them, possessed to a considerable extent a common outlook and common symbols. A particularly telling formulation of this truth comes from Karl Mannheim. Just as an individual knows himself and feels his identity most clearly in certain memorable and crucial experiences of his past which become therefore normative for him, so a society knows itself and orders itself in the light of decisive experiences in its past which illuminate existence. These common memories supply a people with what he calls its "primordial images" and "archetypes." They function as the rallying centers for group loyalties and cohesion. They take on symbolic and mythological development and thus more adequately objectify the faith by which the nation or the age lives. But for our time the archetypes are dimmed or dethroned. The great focuses of our cultural memory have been devaluated, and in their places has arisen a multiplicity of competing values. "God is dead," and the new gods that succeed Him clash at once in sanguinary conflict.

To describe our modern loss of absolutes in philosophy would take us too far afield. The same is true of ethics. What may be appropriately mentioned here is the sway of relativity in education. The presidential address at a recent meeting of the American Association of University Professors argued the advisability of a pluralism of viewpoints and values in the university. It was specifically stated that "anarchy" was the proper intellectual situation for such institutions. Thus the speaker set up his defenses against any and all academic conformism and constraint and safeguarded the utmost freedom of scientific investigation. But at the same time he was in effect excluding any proper guidance of society by the university in a time when that society is falling apart and when the personal costs are incalculable.

The loss of ritual

Another aspect of our situation, closely related to the loss of absolutes, is often referred to as the "loss of ritual." By this we mean much more than neglect of ecclesiastical rites and liturgies. We mean the loss of that communal ceremony and celebration, those feasts and fasts, pomps and jubilees, pilgrimages and holy days, which played so large a part in the older world. These focuses of sanctity in time and place constantly asserted and communicated the deeper sanctions for existence, and kept alive in men a sense of its mysterious and transcendent ground. At the same time they offered themselves as channels of discharge of all that nonrational reservoir of the unconscious in society and the individual which must have expression if it is not to find outlet in alienation and destruction.

The exposure of error in the religious and cultural traditions by science, the skepticism and relativity so long at work in the West, together with the influences of technology making for mechanization, these account in large part for the loss of ritual. "The ceremony of innocence is drowned," as Yeats wrote; "We have the press for wafer: suffrage for circumcision," as Pound put it; a situation which he and others wrongly ascribed to democracy rather than to more fundamental causes. That is, the creative and transfiguring central rites of church and synagogue have given place in our flat and sordid world to the "kitsch" and ugliness of the yellow journal and the pulp literature, life has been despiritualized, and a crass mediocrity has banished all sense of wonder and miracle from existence. In Henry Adams' terms we have the dynamo for the Virgin (or for Aphrodite before the Virgin) as the symbols of power for two different epochs.

The resulting sterility in the inner life of men, the mediocre taste of the Babbitt and the materialism of bourgeois ideals, have their correlatives in the visible face of our civilization, not only in the slums and the mining town and the "country slums," but in the ugliness of suburb and town, manners and crafts, amusements and recreation. This is particularly true of German and Anglo-Saxon countries. Industrialized France and Italy have their wastelands but there is a saving grace of artistic instinct in the Latin peoples, as in Japan and China and India, that defies materialism. In Milton's *Paradise Lost* it is only Mammon, "the least erect of spirits" who is perfectly content to accept hell as a permanent abiding place for the fallen angels. He could live there and not be conscious that there was anything better.

Evidently the loss of ritual, externally at least, is most clearly connected with the mechanization and standardization of life that go with our power civilization. Mass production and technical efficiency treat the sacred pieties of older cultures ruthlessly. Before it all ceremonies and sacred calendars go down— whether the Sunday of the Christian, the Sabbath and high holy days of the Jew, or the Ramadan of the Moslem. And there is little offered in its place. MacIver has well stated the matter: "No ceremonies salute the time-clock and the steam whistle, no hierophants unveil the mysteries of the counting house, no myths attend the tractor and the reaper-binder, no dragons breathe in the open-hearth furnace. For multitudes the art of

living is detached from the business of living and must find
what refuge it can in the now lengthened interval between today's work and tomorrow's."

What T. S. Eliot has from his earliest work so powerfully
stated, he repeats in his more recent work:

> Here is a place of disaffection
> Time before and time after
> In a dim light—
>   Only a flicker
> Over the strained time-ridden faces
> Distracted from distraction by distraction
> Filled with fancies and empty of meaning
> Tumid apathy with no concentration
> Men and bits of paper, whirled by the cold wind
> That blows before and after time,
> Wind in and out of unwholesome lungs.[5]

And Stanley Kunitz in "Reflections by a Mailbox" sees his fellows called to war as:

> . . . the powerful get of a dying age, corrupt
> And passion-smeared, with fluid on their lips,
> As if a soul had been given to petroleum.[6]

Rootlessness

The contemporary picture of disintegration, again, can be
studied in its aspect of the loss of roots. We can relate this to
what has already been said. The loss of absolutes and the loss
of ritual involved, as we saw, the devaluation of tradition. Men
lost their peculiar fatherlands of the soul and became modern
cosmopolites without a history. The deracinated Jew is like the

[5] "Burnt Norton," from *Four Quartets* (New York: Harcourt, Brace
and Company, Inc., 1943). Quoted by permission.

[6] From *Passport to the War* (New York: Henry Holt and Company,
Inc., 1944). Quoted by permission.

deracinated Negro is like the deracinated European is like the deracinated American, as Gertrude Stein might put it. Our homes have no shrines, the Bible is not on our tables, we do not look toward Mecca or Jerusalem or the setting sun. We live in and for today. Our roots in older times are cut.

But the loss of roots has other aspects. For one thing multitudes of men have lost their connection with earth and mother nature. They are born and die in the city, they spend their days in the factory, the mine or the office. They have no living contact with the soil or the processes of nature. Between them and the living earth is the cement and the asphalt; between them and the stars are the skyscrapers and the apartment houses. They have only an indirect awareness of the procession of the seasons. It is no wonder that the ancient seasonal rituals have lost their hold, the feasts of solstice and equinox and the agricultural feasts of sowing and harvest. These multitudes are troglodytes in the artificial caverns of the machine age and the megalopolis. Something primordial is lost here. Even "natural religion" is precluded in such conditions, and natural religion is the basis of higher religion.

But more important is the loss of roots in community. Such conditions strike at community bonds even more effectively than at natural pieties and sentiments. Man is a social animal and his health depends on the psychological securities of the neighborhood and the tribe. We do not need to repeat what so many sociologists have said about the loss of community in modern life. The family itself, the basic molecule of society, is dissociated. The organic bonds that guarantee man status are broken, and we have an atomistic culture. The emancipation from feudal or patriarchal or rural patterns exacts its price in the depersonalization of man.

With this term, the "depersonalization" of man, we have

reached the most significant and comprehensive datum of our analysis. This is the end result of our cultural disintegration, and it is at this point that efforts at reintegration take their rise and can be understood. But first note just what it means and what it costs are. It means that men are out of organic relations, isolated, both in the social and the spiritual sense, and that though they are integers in various power hierarchies, yet their field of responsible choice and their freedom of personal action have rapidly diminished. Current discussion has many terms for this "little man." It speaks of his "anonymity"; he has lost his name like the heroes of Kafka's novels. He is a "cowed (intimidated) cypher." In the economic context he is a robot, in the military, an expendable conscript. He has a sense of impotence over against the impersonal forces that underlie the business cycle or the outbreak of war. Or he is only too conscious of the personal authority of the dictator, the business czar or the boss. For the *Führer* in war has his counterpart in peace. Dylan Thomas dramatizes the fact of controlling power in a few hands or a single hand:

> The hand that signed the paper felled a city;
> Five sovereign fingers taxed the breath,
> Doubled the globe of dead and halved a country;
> These five kings did a king to death.[7]

Psychologically and subjectively this modern man is the man without a face, who struggles for the sense of his identity and for status. The experience of isolation passes into that of alienation and neurosis. Not having organic personal relations by which to secure himself, not having a field of personal action, he becomes passive. He loses his power of resistance and con-

[7] From *The World I Breathe* (Norfolk, Conn.: New Directions Press, 1939), p. 47. Quoted by permission.

sistency. Aldous Huxley in *Point Counter Point* describes such a state: "His mind was amoeboid, 'like a sea of spiritual protoplasm,' capable of flowing in all directions. . . . At different times in his life and even at the same moment he had filled the most various molds . . . where was the self to which he could be loyal?"[8]

Much of modern literature reflects or studies these aspects of modern man. Two themes recur and can be illustrated by Franz Kafka's two best-known novels. One of them is that of the search for status, for belonging, for community. In *The Castle*, Kafka pictures an outsider, an alien, who tries to establish himself in a humble position in a village. The symbolic narration has a nightmare quality suggestive of the anxiety and anguish with which the hero seeks to escape from his insecurity and solitude. In the allegory of the story he stands not only for the insecure white collar employee of modern bureaucratic society seeking to secure himself economically, but more especially for modern man generally in his spiritual lostness under powers that veil themselves. The "castle" in this case, in or through which he must acquire his status, denies access to itself yet tantalizes with promises and concessions soon countermanded. This craving for place and recognition in the common life recurs in most of the major writers of today in the prominence given to the theme of the exile, the alien, the wanderer. We need only instance the significant place taken in contemporary works of Ulysses (Joyce), Joseph in Egypt (Thomas Mann), Ahasuerus—The Wandering Jew (Joyce again), Oedipus (Camus and T. S. Eliot's *Family Reunion*).

Kafka's *The Trial* brings out another aspect of depersonalization, that of impotence in the face of the social and spiritual

[8] *Point Counter Point* (New York: Harper & Brothers, 1928). Cited in Slochauer, *op. cit.*, p. 34.

hierarchies of our day. It is true that we have spoken of the freedom of the modern man. But emancipation from medieval authority and other traditions nevertheless in the long run left him confronted by the insoluble problems of existence and those immitigable necessities which make no concessions to his desires. And these very emancipations smoothed the way for new political and economic tyrannies. The theme of *The Trial* is well known. The hero, "Joseph K.," an innocent employee, wakes up one morning to find himself under arrest and he is never able to clear himself or shake off the jurisdiction over his case of the mysterious but almighty authorities that indict him. His ambiguous situation and his endless expedients in the effort to justify and free himself constitute an allegory of original sin. Yet on another level we have a portrayal of the dependence and bondage of middle-class man over against the power centers of modern society. Kafka uses this latter theme, however, chiefly as a vehicle of the generalized sense of guilt and of disquietude that grips men. An expression of this on a less esoteric level is found in a poem of Kenneth Fearing's, "Confession Overheard in a Subway," in which everyman gives voice to what is universally repressed:

> You will ask how I came to be eavesdropping, in the first place.
> The answer is, I was not.
> The man who confessed to these several crimes (call him John Doe) spoke into my right ear on a crowded subway train, while the man whom he addressed (call him Richard Roe) stood at my left.
> Thus, I stood between them, and they talked, or sometimes shouted, quite literally straight through me.
> How could I help but overhear?
> Perhaps I might have gone away to some other strap.
> But the aisles were full.

Besides, I felt, for some reason, curious.

"I do not deny my guilt," said John Doe. "My own, first,
　　and after that my guilty knowledge of still further
　　guilt.
I have counterfeited often, and successfully.
I have been guilty of ignorance and talking with convic-
　　tion. Of intolerable wisdom and keeping silent.
Through carelessness, or cowardice, I have shortened the
　　lives of better men. And the name for that is murder.
All my life I have been a receiver of stolen goods."
"Personally, I always mind my own business," said
　　Richard Roe. "Sensible people don't get into those
　　scrapes."

"Guilt," said John is always and everywhere nothing less
　　than guilt.
I have always, at all times, been a willing accomplice of
　　the crass and the crude.
I have overheard, daily, the smallest details of con-
　　spiracies against the human race, vast in their ulti-
　　mate scope, and conspired, daily, to launch my own.
You have heard of innocent men who died in the chair.
　　It was my avarice that threw the switch.
I helped, and I do not deny it, to nail that guy to the
　　cross, and shall continue to help.
Look into my eyes, you can see the guilt.
Look at my face, my hair, my very clothing, you will see
　　guilt written plainly everywhere.
Guilt of the flesh. Of the soul. Of eating, when others do
　　not. Of breathing and laughing and sleeping.
I am guilty of what? Of guilt. Guilty of guilt, that is all,
　　and enough."[9]

The loss of absolutes, the loss of ritual, the loss of roots (in
nature and community) suggest then the character of present-

[9] From *Afternoon of a Pawn-Broker and Other Poems* (New York:
Harcourt, Brace and Company, 1943). Quoted by permission.

day culture and we have noted some of the costs involved. This situation evidently sets special tasks for the Church. And we must not forget that the Church itself suffers' the inroads of these conditions. We would, however, recur to a caution we have hitherto expressed. It is too simple to see the factors and the conditions as all negative. Much disintegration of old patterns and authorities is to be desired. There will be no gain, however, if the new patterns that replace them are unbaptized and inhumane, whatever the names (democracy! the Four Freedoms!) with which they may cover themselves. Much of the disintegration is desirable. But the *state* of disintegration is not desirable. Yet we should also note that human nature has a marvelous faculty of redeeming its worst liabilities and conditions. This mechanization, this rootlessness, this neuroticism of today do not, even so, starve out all affection, all natural impulse, all colorfulness and sanity by any means. The heart vibrates and the soul breathes even in a world where so much of its oxygen is removed. Indeed, as we move about in our age our temptation is to suppose that our fellows are in the large majority healthy, and that this world is not a sick world. After all, we say, this ruling middle class has its code of decency, its civic ideals and its humane responses to a neighbor's needs. The standard of living is the best in the world's history. Parents love their children and every large city has its symphony orchestra! Union members wear flowers in their buttonholes at their dances! But the surface of life should not deceive us. And the moving power of human nature to affirm itself against all blights and plagues should not blind us to the whole picture. We live in a tragic time.

3. REINTEGRATION:
NEW ORDERS AND NEW CULTS

The picture of our culture includes not only the end results
of disintegration but also many efforts at reintegration, some of
them well advanced. Nature abhors a vacuum here also, and
when old gods go, new gods arrive. In one aspect we may say
that a period of analysis and criticism has brought forth its
inevitable reaction in varied impulses toward synthesis and
holism. As Fichte already recognized: "We began to philoso-
phize out of exuberance and therefore deprived ourselves of innocence. We noted our nakedness, and since then we philoso-
phize out of our need for redemption." We see the same picture
whether we look at philosophy, traditions, cults or communities.
New faiths replace old; moribund traditions are revived; the
multitudes, famished for significant symbols, flock to new rituals; and new or revived herd movements attract the individual
terrified by his isolation. The appeal of the new loyalties is
broadcast and amplified by the novel techniques of propaganda.
Moreover, the power of resistance to false guides and irrational
solutions has already been broken down by despair and enerva-
tion.

But we do not need to explain the emergence of such new
forms and faiths. The depths of human nature are perennially
explosive. Man is in a condition of perennial gestation. He
brings forth dynamic creations which are as often destructive
as otherwise. Tradition and ritual, religion and art, are the
world-old dykes, or channels of these volcanic forces, and
where they are suicidely removed the way is open to devastation. Those who rest upon the pleasant assurance that man has
a divine spark in him that allies him to God sometimes con-
fuse the divine spark with the blazing faggot that also burns in

him. Let rationalism, idealism or romanticism take notice. Fortunately, some of the new impulses toward order and community today are disabused of such illusions and are constructive.

New collectivisms

The flight from disintegration manifests itself particularly in the impulse toward community. Even though often blind and exploited this feature of our time is to be valued. It is one aspect of the "flight from freedom," i.e., from excess of freedom. The uprooted and isolated and depersonalized masses awaken to the danger of their situation, and troop toward any standard. Yet the banners that are lifted are no chance emblems. They represent profound hungers and coercive if partial aspirations. For the proletariat: communism. For the middle class: fascism. And these two merge easily with racism or nationalism. Thus we get emotional ideologies that have the explosive force of religion, and they impregnate in various ways our whole culture. Literature and art are the first to register and to react to these intoxicating fumes and vapors which course through the world. But the point here is that these movements emerge as communities, destroying old community bonds and creating new ones around conceptions and loyalties incommensurate with the old. The minds of their devotees are impervious to our reasonings or appeals. And what we forget is that we ourselves, all unawares, are infected, so that even our best ideals are subtly corrupted. "Democracy" itself is misconceived and becomes a blind and a pretext for undemocratic attitudes. It can be made into an idol as we read into it a guarantee of whatever *status quo* or privilege our own interests dictate.

One redeeming aspect of this new collectivization is found in the numerous sporadic experiments in communal life and co-operatives, jealous to safeguard the true autonomy of the person, which have appeared both within and outside of the churches. Corresponding to these is the even more manifest summons to brotherhood and true personal "meeting" in contemporary literature. MacLeish defines love as the "pole star for this year." Miss Rukeyser ironically describes the weakness of love in a world of aliens: "We wound past armies of strangers, waving love's thin awkward plant among a crowd of salesmen." John Bunker sees a revolt of the masses animated paradoxically by a ruthless love:

> We must cleanse the earth
> With sorrow and hate . . .
> But mostly with love,
> Love pitiless, unrelenting, omnipotent,
> Love hungry with a great hunger—
> Love for mankind.[10]

And the term "love" recurs through the work of Auden:

> O every day in sleep and labor
> Our life and death are with our neighbor,
> And love illuminates again
> The city and the lion's den
> The world's great rage, the travel of young men.[11]

Resurgent vitalities: aesthetic and religious

The flight from disintegration appears again—and here also often in a suspect form—in new mythologies and cults, this time of the individual rather than of the group. This is a long story. We have in mind chiefly all those irrational expressions that have arisen as a protest to the mechanization and sterility of modern life. Our age has had its pseudo prophets who have

[10] From *Revolt* (New York: Campion Press, 1940), p. 5. Quoted by permission.

[11] W. H. Auden, "New Year's Letter," *op. cit.*, p. 316. Quoted by permission.

voiced one or another form of primitivism or vitalism or private mysticism. Arthur Koestler has spoken of "the Yogi and the commissar." Let the Commissar stand as the representative of the totalitarian community described above. The Yogi stands for what we have here in view. Sometimes, indeed, direct if falsified importations of Hindu or Buddhist influence are present. Fundamentally, however, we have to do with neopagan impulses derived from the unbaptized vitalities of the West. These can be serviceable, but too often by excess of reaction they take the form of pride and irresponsibility. Nietzsche, on one side of his Protean nature, is a fountainhead of this phenomenon. D. H. Lawrence, though widely traduced, exemplifies it. There are about us countless inarticulate men and women who in their intimate values belong to the following of the Swamis. Their resistance to Christianity is not merely indifference or the love of pleasure as we tend to think. They follow false gods. In another age they would have been with the followers of Isis and Cybele, with the gnostics or the astrologers. Indeed, some of them are today. Likewise beneath the bohemianism and aestheticism of many sophisticated groups one discovers similar cults and pieties. Yet even here the baffling character of modern culture appears in the strange intermixture of valuable elements with the spurious. So many healthful influences continue in our time from the past that even the errorists are partly blessed by them. And a resort to the primitive in impulse and outlook is often a necessary if dangerous way of renewal of desiccated arts or a drought-stricken culture.

Lawrence was led to burst the strait jacket of middle-class nonconformist mores and conceptions where they had become most unlovely and constricting—namely, in such an industralized area as his native Nottinghamshire. But his testimony ultimately took on the character of a generalized criticism of civilization.

In Mexico and New Mexico, in Italy and Sardinia he found culture patterns that restored to him a true sense of life's mystery and power. Gauguin initiated the quest of the painters for a more immediate contact with unspoiled nature. It was not only that he sought the cultural primitivism of Samoa but that like his followers among various schools of modern artists and writers he declared for the sensibility of the child and even the infant. The freshness of such naïve experience would more than compensate for the loss of sophistication where the latter had become cerebral or corrupt. Thus he wrote: "Barbarism means to me a return to youth. I went way back, farther back than the horses of the Parthenon . . . as far back as the *dada* of my infancy, and my toy wooden horse."[12] A more recent example is that of the American sculptor, John Flanagan. He gave up almost entirely working with the human figure. Modern man, so he judged, is obsessed with man, with himself, with his sick soul and his own body. It is a kind of narcissism. Better to turn away from man and contemplate the natural world animate or inanimate. ". . . man should not praise himself, but kneel in adoration for the vastness of the creation." Here is objectivity, freedom, health. Flanagan's significant work is almost entirely made up of small-scale studies of animals and birds. Something of the mystery of creation reappears in this approach which combines that of the scientist and the artist. In a somewhat similar mood Robinson Jeffers turns from the corruption of man to the unstained and inhuman chastities of the Sierras and the western ocean, and to the purity of the rock and the wild creatures.

But primitivism and pseudoprimitivism have taken on many forms, some of them highly sophisticated. In Jeffers, in a variety of forms which it is unwise to attempt to reduce to a

[12] Cited in Slochauer, *op. cit.*, p. 132.

philosophy—since it is a poet and not a philosopher who speaks
—there results a Titanism which from an immense height
surveys, arraigns and prophecies evil ("Cassandra") for our
civilization and our nation. In Aldous Huxley and in Gerald
Heard an attempt is made in various ways to renew the mystical
tradition in Christianity or to fertilize it with themes and practices from the Orient. There is good in all these attempts to
cure our ills, and Christianity at its best has known how to
encourage and sanctify both man's natural religion and his
pagan traditions. But it has also known how to judge them and
to be severe in selection and rejection, "bringing every thought
(valuation) into captivity to the obedience of Christ," submitting *eros* to *agape*, and refusing all intoxications and heady
gnosticisms which in the name of freedom open the door to
irresponsibility. It is forewarned out of long experience that
the irrationalism of the private cult easily passes into the
irrationalism of soil or blood or state. Man's nature is so
extravagant and prodigal that even the primary and healthy
currents toward fullness of life and creation that arise in the
soul too easily run in the channels of sensuality, self-aggrandize-
ment or power.

The Negro in the conditions of city life today offers a good
example of the clash between native impulse and the factors
that smother and repress these, an example all the more reveal-
ing in view of his greater gifts of spontaneity. Gwendolyn
Brooks tellingly evokes the instinct for the dramatic and the
colorful of this people so harshly inhibited by the character of
our culture, and in "The Sundays of Satin-Legs Smith"[13] she
is really generalizing about multitudes today whether black or

[13] *A Street in Bronzeville* (New York: Harper & Brothers, 1945), p. 26.
Quoted by permission.

white. Satin-Legs' starved aspiration toward richness and splendor finds its inadequate compensation in his:

> wonder suits in yellow and in wine,
> Sarcastic greens and zebra-striped cobalt . . .

And,

> Here are hats
> Like bright umbrellas; and hysterical ties
> Like narrow banners for some gathering war.

But the immitigable limitations on all such hungers are only too clear and too cruel, limitations, that is, in such an order or disorder as ours. The "gold impulse" is thwarted:

> Below the tinkling trade of little coins
> The gold impulse not possible to show
> Or spend. Promise piled over and betrayed.

Is it any wonder that the betrayed impulse turns to some side-tracked or destructive expression in private fad, group orgy or mad ideology, and finally violence? Such a culture confronts Christianity with needs at various points. When the chain of evil reaches outward expression in violence and conflict, Christianity has to formulate its views of the maintenance of public order and the relative rights of competing power groups. At the more fundamental level of the underlying conditions Christianity has a twofold task. It must criticize the society and the culture that thus stifle the growth of youth toward adequate emotional and spiritual expression and offer it the ritual and drama and depth that belong to it. And it must know meanwhile how to "save" the individual and the family even where the damning general conditions continue.

The same situation which prompts the aesthetic and religious cults of which we have been speaking also goes far to explain many more generalized features of our culture. Special mention should be made here of the character of amusements and recreation in our society. What is called the "jazz age" has passed through several successive phases, but the febrile satisfactions bestowed continue to illuminate the background of a mechanized and rationalized existence. The special forms taken by the drama, the moving picture, the novel and periodical or ephemeral publication tell their story. They speak eloquently of the omnipresent demands, whether for excitement, escape, distraction or partisanship. The accent in many of our social expressions, as witness sports, and performances and exhibitions of many kinds, is on heightened forms of the dramatic, on the shock valve; and alcohol, sensuality and gambling, one or more, are associated with most of our recreation. The depersonalized psyche, the numbed and enervated worker, requires high-tension stimuli to recover a transient awareness of his own identity.

Return to tradition

The flight from disintegration and rootlessness, finally, takes a third form in a return to tradition. It is as though the advance scouts and echelons realized that they had gotten out too far ahead of the main army. They therefore fall back to re-establish contact. Here we have a return to absolutes that are defined by history. Thus we have neo-orthodoxies of various schools. Among these neo-humanism has the greatest difficulty in lifting its voice in these days but we still hear appeals to the sanity of Socrates, Erasmus and Goethe. Educators fight a defensive battle for Greek and Latin, and now hope to take advantage of the panic induced by these catastrophic times to restore the humane arts and letters to their former place. But this kind of traditionalism is doubly weak today. It starts with the handicap of little direct knowledge from the inside of the new forces of today, and it lacks an adequate philosophy. Either it represents only an aesthetic eclecticism or if it appeals to the *philosophia perennis* it too evidently stops short of the authoritative appeal of either Aquinas or Calvin.

Neo-Thomism and the various forms of return to the Reformation are, indeed, live options today. The former also has its various shadings. On one side it merges imperceptibly with an academic humanism such as we have just mentioned. The term is loosely and mistakenly assigned to any who appeal to the great distinction of natural and supernatural revelation or who invoke reason, virtue and the soul in intellectual or political discussion. Neo-Thomism proper, however, requires a grave intellectual decision or series of decisions, in essential agreement with Aristotle and Aquinas, which set aside perhaps much of the error of the modern world but therewith also much of its experience. Neo-Thomism is only the most articulate and influential form of appeal of non-Protestant Christian philosophy. There are Catholics who appeal rather to Duns Scotus, and others, in this case Anglicans, who appeal to a Platonistic theology. The great question with all of these is whether they are simply and solely reaction or whether they represent a serious coming-to-terms with modern experience and thought.

Protestant neo-orthodoxy whether on its Calvinist or Lutheran wings raises the same question. For our diagnosis of contemporary culture we are not concerned first of all with the theological issues. The significance for us of Barthianism in its various senses is whether it constitutes a repudiation of modern experience or an attempt to digest and incorporate it. We should not at any time deprecate the repossession of tradition. But tradition should be repossessed in the light of the present. The past becomes a safe guide only where by a spiritual effort it is comprehended as part of a larger present. We make ourselves contemporaries of those that have gone before so that their experiences and decisions become our responsibility along with the experiences and decisions of today.[14]

But too much of the neo-orthodoxy as of the Neo-Thomism of today is in the bad sense reactionary. The past remains the past and men imitate it or accept its authority by way of a bondage rather than a responsible renewal. This kind of grasping for absolutes in a day of relativity, while it offers a specious refuge, is no real solution of the problems of depersonalization and deracination. Here again, as with capitulation to the Commissar or the Yogi, men only find status by acceptance of new overlords whether political or spiritual.

What should be added here, however, is that the great faiths in their legitimate forms, do have the character of absolutes. But these absolutes derive their authority from the immediate apprehension of God and the living consent of the soul and not from any more concrete or objectified authority such as institution, creed or book. The latter are, indeed, essential carriers or vehicles of the faith but the faith itself must remain personal. More adequate symbols and rites of the Christian faith, suggestive both of its depth and of its ancient continuity, are a paramount claim upon religious reform today. But where these take the place of personal faith and responsibility,

[14] We are aware that Barthianism proposes a kind of contemporaneity in experience and decision for all men of all times. There is a great truth in this existential transcendence of history. The trouble is that it is not sufficiently "existential" in the other sense of the term. For the actual and diverse experience of men in different circumstances and times is not concretely envisaged as conditioning the religious problem. Strict Barthianism thus makes an abstraction of history and takes on a gnostic, i.e., heterodox character.

there Christianity today is confronted by false absolutisms even in the Church itself.

We have sought to portray the disorder of our time and to trace its origin in intellectual and cultural influences of past and present. We should not, however, assign too great a significance to the role of ideas and movements, or let ourselves be beguiled into a deterministic view of these evils. The moral factor is primary.

> Accurate scholarship can
> Unearth the whole offense
> From Luther until now
> That has driven a culture mad,
> Find what occurred at Linz,
> What huge imago made
> A psychopathic god:
> I and the public know
> What all school children learn,
> Those to whom evil is done
> Do evil in return.[15]

The hurts and costs of contemporary life are deeply conditioned by prevailing faiths and unfaiths. Multitudes of men grow and live under the sway of dogmas and under the tyranny of circumstances that limit their responsibility, induce spiritual maladies, and provoke them to fraud or violence. But each human being possesses an area of freedom and action which constitutes liberty. To this Christianity must address its message and its demand, at the same time that it passes judgment on the pagan structures and valuations which limit that freedom.

[15] W. H. Auden, "September 1, 1939," *op. cit.*, p. 57. Quoted by permission.

Further Reading

BERDYAEV, NICHOLAS. *The End of Our Time*. New York: Sheed & Ward, Inc., 1933.

HOPPER, STANLEY. *The Crisis of Faith*. New York: Abingdon-Cokesbury Press, 1944.

KAFKA, FRANZ. *The Castle*. New York: Alfred A Knopf, 1930.

————. *The Trial*. New York: Alfred A. Knopf, 1937.

KOESTLER, ARTHUR. *The Yogi and the Commissar*. New York: The Macmillan Company, 1945.

LUCCOCK, HALFORD E. *American Mirror*. New York: The Macmillan Company, 1940.

SLOCHAUER, HARRY. *No Voice is Wholly Lost*. New York: Creative Age Press, 1945.

TRUEBLOOD, ELTON. *The Predicament of Modern Man*. New York: Harper & Brothers, 1945.

7

SECULARISM IN THE CHURCH

James H. Nichols

1. Protestantism in American culture. Its "lost provinces." Impersonal relations. Political ethics. Economic ethics. 2. Personal relationships. Racism. Family and sex relations. 3. Impoverishment and irrelevance of church activities. 4. Renaissance of Christian social responsibility. The recovery of Christian community and discipline.

THE chapters of this volume have designed to single out certain salient aspects of the civilization in which we have been set to fulfill our Christian vocations. They do not claim to be exhaustive but simply indicate areas where problems are posed. Since they are all aspects of liberal capitalistic civilization, or its transformation, they have relevance to the whole world situation, for at least in the most external political and economic and technological relations all the continents and islands are now bound together. Our focus, nevertheless, is in the peculiar equilibrium of forces in North America, where contrasts are not so sharp nor the revloutionary transitions of the age so explicit as in Europe or Asia. Here humanizing and moderating influences complicate and obscure the dynamics of industrial society as revealed in naked imperialism to the "younger churches" of Asia, or as diverted into new political and

spiritual channels by new secular faiths in Europe. The deper-
sonalizing and irreligious aspects of our technological civilization, on the other hand, are as devastating to the ancient
religions of Africa and Asia as to our own, and Buddhism,
Confucianism, Hinduism and Islam all confront with us the
new mass men who respect only efficiency yet are readily converted to new secular absolutisms. These problems may not be
central in all situations today, but they will probably all be
universally recognizable.

For the present writer there remains the task of retracing
some of this ground to make explicit and to summarize the
particular challenge this civilization presents for the Christian
life. The perennial paradoxes and the ultimate nature of Christian ethics are not here our concern, but rather the unique and
peculiar forms in which our moral life is determined by the
crisis in which we must live. We speak, in the first place, for
and out of the culture of American Protestantism, which is in
many ways the largest, most compact, most firmly entrenched
Protestant culture of today's world. We should not be ungrate-
ful that we are the inheritors of probably the most successful
aggression of Christianity on culture in all its history, the
sectarian and Calvinist permeation of modern political and
economic and social ethics. We should not permit ourselves to
forget the notable vitality of American Protestantism down to
our own day, particularly as seen in its tremendous missionary
expansion, its remarkable social impact, both here and abroad,
and its determined if sometimes naïve impulse to church reunion. It is our destiny, nevertheless, to live in the ebb tide of
that aggression, when the practices of our common life still
flow in channels cut by religious consecration, but when those
springs no longer run clear, and alien currents sweep the
courses. American culture, and with it too much of American
Protestantism, has become nearly paralyzed by its moral uncer-

tainty. Our money and our courageous but bewildered young men won a war we do not as a people yet understand. Our traditional ideals are so compromised by economic injustice, color caste and incipient imperialism that we have lost our sense of destiny or vocation. The masses of our people, deprived of religious roots, are fed largely on unrealizable dreams of personal advantage and comfort, and their resentments in depression will be tinder to demagogues. It is time, it is perhaps too late, for American Protestantism to withdraw to the sources of its vocation and recover its capacities for judgment and leadership. Just so the great medieval attempt to master civilization for Christianity ran out into the secular sands from the days of Thomas Aquinas, and the Church had to be disengaged and rediscovered.

A world has died and the cultural strata least aware of it, who cling to their specious securities in irresponsible complacency, are the very groups which set the tone of American Protestantism. Their clerical leaders who think at all dare not face their thoughts. They know they are impotent; they are shepherding a flock of chickens about in a barnyard still unscathed in a battlefield, seeking to persuade themselves of safety in familiar routines. They and their churches are next to futile amid the great social forces of modern life, and they know it in their hearts. And around these frightened little flocks stands the ring of cold unsmiling faces who ask for truth and justice *now*, the working classes, the emancipated intellectuals, the veterans who have learned how to tell verbiage from reality. In these and similar groups more exposed to the currents of the day, there is often to be found more insight into our present predicament than is known in the churches. For a few minutes at a time we believe and are horror-struck at what is happening to our civilization, then we cross again the thresholds of our routine and this wildness slips to the edge of our consciousness and becomes unreal and impossible amid all the familiar smells and ritual. We are no longer the respected leaders of our civilization; we are a minority. But we cannot believe it and we therefore avoid all decisive actions which would demonstrate how slight is the sufferance which permits our continued respectability.

1. THE LOST PROVINCES: IMPERSONAL RELATIONSHIPS

We must begin with a review of the long series of defensive actions, or of mere retreats, by which one after another of the areas of our common life have come to deny the rights of Christian ethics even in principle. A description of these cumulative retrenchments can be usefully outlined in terms of "lost provinces" of the common life. The cartography of these provinces knows one fundamental boundary: that between those social relationships which are personal, such as those of family, neighborhood, servant (or hired hand) and employer relations, small business, school and cultural associations; and, on the other hand, those which are impersonal, those ties which link us at some distance with several million Chinese, or even several million Americans we have never seen and never will see, and those which bind us in economic relationships with all sorts of people in all manner of places. In both cases we have to reckon with our incorrigible urge to dominate and use others, but with personal relations a certain mutuality and forgiveness is possible which scarcely exists as between our massive objectified egoisms in anonymous corporation or state actions. Their deeds are neutral, cold and ruthless, unaccessible to mercy or more than the barest minimum of moral insight. The contrast has been brilliantly dramatized for us in Reinhold Niebuhr's *Moral Man and Immoral Society*, and whatever reservations we may have as to the accuracy of that motto, we can be grateful for the emphasis on the fact that in the world of the larger impersonal organizations of power, major decisions are habitually taken in our name in complete carelessness of Christian ethics. How can we really believe that the God of Jesus Christ rules or is served in the world of states and big business?

The analogy of lost provinces must be guarded from an interpretation which is too widely accepted, namely, that we Christians are not responsible for what is done by the great cold bureaucracies of economic and political power. The lost provinces are still inhabited to a large extent by nominal Christians and what is done in them is done by Christians. I have never killed a man with my own hands but for years I have been paying something like eighty cents out of the dollar in taxes to hire men to do it for me. More than once in the last war I caught myself enjoying a bestial satisfaction in reading the account of some military achievement. Certain atrocities committed by the military forces of the United States truly expressed vicious impulses of mine which I would never have dared confess to myself in a personal role. Morally and financially I contributed to very evil deeds, which were compounded of this evil in me and its counterpart in many others, few of whom would conceivably indulge such deviltry on their sole responsibility. But we did it. In the competition of great industrial and financial corporations, again, no nice ethical scruples are to be expected. If one is unwilling to injure or cheat employees, stockholders or the consumer to the extent to which one's rival will go, then one must abandon the field to him. I sat on no board and voted no unethical policy, but I loaned my money to men who did, and wisely asked no questions. I accepted my share of stolen goods in gratitude and devoted it to the Christian purpose of educating my children to serve humanity. Or again I am not a member of the real estate owner's association of my neighborhood which maintains restrictive covenants against Negroes and thereby systematically debauches hundreds of children, condemning them to tuberculosis, syphilis, degradation and crime. I contribute neither funds nor moral support, but whatever shame I feel I unquestionably profit in comfort and status from the oppression of the Negro. These provinces are lost because we Christians submit singly and helplessly to the principalities and powers who rule us in them.

International relations

The first province, that of international relations, whose ominous stirrings we watch with dull terror, has increasingly cast off any ethical restraints since the end of the Wars of Religion in the seventeenth century. At least in ideal, Church and empire had exercised some moral authority over the political rulers of the high Middle Ages in their mutual relations. After the Reformation and the Wars of Religion the new autonomous sovereign states of Europe were still united in a comparable moral community as Grotius and other pioneers of Protestant humanism replaced Roman canon law by the modern discipline of international law. While the *curia* protested its exclusion from the arbiter's seat among the states, the principles of natural law were common to Protestant and Roman Catholic states and this Christianized stoicism gave some direction to the Christian conscience in international affairs. This pattern was still the moral basis of the League of Nations in Anglo-Saxon countries in our own day, and it has been one of the weaknesses of the United States in international affairs to suppose that such Christian humanism is still a generally accepted idiom. The violent repudiation of such restraints by Germany and Italy in our own generation and the rise to dominant power of nominally anti-Christian Russia, together with the likely emergence of great new states in Asia with no such presuppositions, radically change our situation. The historical least common denominator is now gone and we find ourselves confronting non-Christian states (if not ourselves citizens of such a one) just as Christendom as a whole confronted Greco-Roman paganism in the ancient world or Islam in the medieval. We have almost certainly progressed beyond the level of intercultural ethics displayed in the Crusades and Thomas Aquinas' recommendation to keep no faith with heretics. But the achievement of a common ground with absolutist political faiths like Islam, Marxism or the rising nationalisms of Asia will be one of the desperately important problems of Christian ethics in the next generation even assuming that America herself can still be guided by any moral considerations.

Politics

This last reflection brings us to another major type of non-personal ethical relationship in which our civilization presents us with new crises, and Christian ethics has suffered defeat. In the Middle Ages and Reformation centuries, emperors, kings and princes were consciously organs of the ecclesiastico-political body. They ruled by *divine* right, and recognized a concomitant Christian moral responsibility with a fidelity varying with personal character. In the seventeenth and eighteenth centuries, the established churches, Catholic, Anglican, Lutheran, and in our generation, Eastern Orthodox, relinquished their control of state power and social discipline only under compulsion, but the governmental elites, and the middle classes on which they were everywhere increasingly dependent, admitted ever less ecclesiastical regulation of politics. It should be observed, however, that the transition was not simply to baldly secular ends, although it has often seemed such in Roman Catholic and Lutheran countries. The shock troops of the liberal revolutions in Holland and England were recruited among convinced Christians of the Puritan and Reformed tradition who had effected a new synthesis of Christian humanist political theory. They broke the ground and set the pattern, nerved by a religious responsibility and moral discipline their emulators in France and Germany scarcely shared. In Switzerland, Holland, Britain and the United States liberalism and democracy have thus had a solidity never achieved in Germany or Roman Catholic countries. Eastern Orthodoxy, German Lutheranism and Roman Catholicism have been unable to discipline the individual citizen to a personal religious responsibility in a free government. They have lived by clerical and police authority, and when that was repudiated, there was no discipline among citizens trained by them to maintain the vitality of republican government. They have not been politically creative in the modern world, unless contemporary totalitarianism be counted to them, but have simply consummated an alliance of ecclesiastical authority with the traditional pattern of a society of status and insisted on obedience and order, each man in his station. Christianity could with equal or better right be assimilated to the stoic strain of revolutionary natural law with its egalitarianism or at least universal responsibility. Some such synthesis was the great Puritan contribution to political ethics in the modern world and has been the most important Christian achievement in modern politics. It is the justification for the current American confusion of Christianity and political democracy.

In our day, however, this Protestant synthesis in political theory is itself dangerously strained by the same pressures of industrialized society which have quite shattered democratic forms in virtually all states outside this religious tradition. Since this present crisis results largely from new developments in the third major category of nonpersonal ethical relationships, those of large scale economic organization, we may defer discussion of it until we have analyzed the problem of Christian economic ethics.

Economics

The analogy of a lost province is perhaps most frequently applied to this latter area of social life. There seems to be a complete antithesis between, e.g., the moral controls over usury, master and workman relations, the just price, of the medieval and Reformation centuries and the almost amoral and inhuman versions of laissez-faire capitalism which were widely influential in the middle generation of the last century and remain so today at least in certain colonial areas. From the late seventeenth century until the end of the nineteenth economic theory developed in increasing independence from ethics. Modern economic organization has been informed less by community needs under moral direction than by systematic avarice, or at least by a compulsion to maximum productivity with only the most imperfect and indirect guidance toward welfare by what the economists significantly call "effective" demand. The banker's confession that "in the world of finance it makes no difference whatever whether a man is a Christian or not" holds for many or most types of large scale business.

The impact on community and personality of the social organizations created to serve this final end of productive efficiency is perhaps the most pervasive antireligious influence in our civilization. With machines as instruments of control over nature we could make our peace, although even here there are certain spiritual values lost which come only to men who live close to organic things, the seasons and the soil and animal creation. But a mechanized society, a society which values and rewards men only in terms of their technical efficiency, is a moral wilderness. For this we force "unneeded" farmers off the soil, suck away the children of villages and towns to live in warrens in the cities and to labor as "hands" in the factories or as clerks in the economic bureaucracies. Family and neighborhood associations dissolve, the group life with common symbols and traditions capable of cultivation to high art is scattered around metropolitan centers, its members isolated among those of alien tongue. Technical advances make possible a complete mobility of society, so that enduring relationships cannot be assumed and common life is reduced to temporary and tentative dealings on the minimum level while individuals constantly shuttle about to serve the mechanical requirements of the productive structure. In this insecurity and isolation we fear and huddle and become mass men, but still without fundamental trust in one another.

This is the portrait of the average American today with his insecurity and his conservatism. Raised on the hope of great rewards for individual enterprise, he finds in fact, although he may not grasp it as a generalization, that he actually lives in an economy of "modified monopoly" where only a very small and rapidly decreasing proportion of men can hope for great rewards for individual enterprise. The great majority of Americans, eight or nine out of every ten, are, and will always remain, employees, "stuck to a job" which neither fulfills their creative urges nor compensates for routine by a salary in any way commensurate with the American dream. With a population no

longer increasing and the constant contraction of markets over-
seas the whole economy consolidates, crystallizing social
classes with it. The growth of great economic states within the
state, however, has continued at a rapidly increasing rate until
the very constitution of representative government stands in
danger. The secret anonymous government of a few hundred
corporate managers, responsible to no community voice or
organ but controlling the livelihood of millions, steadily consolidates its power in spite of all governmental efforts to break
up monopoly and restore free enterprise. The handful of men
who control the policies of just one of the great American
corporations are masters of a productive capacity equal to that
of all Britain, France and Belgium on the eve of the last war.
Decisions which those men, or others like them in command of
similar empires, may make in one day are often vastly more
significant for the course of public affairs and the destiny of
millions than the business enacted in legislative halls by the
duly-elected representatives of the people.

The issue of the political and moral responsibility of this
hidden government of the nation's economic life is the focus
of the challenge now confronting the economic and the political
ethic of Protestantism. A cursory survey would seem to indicate prevailing confusion and impotence before the problem.
The whole economic ethic of Protestantism, which provided the
moral asceticism and devotion to a task beyond the requirements of consumption which vastly speeded the initial rationalization of modern society, today plays into the hands of those
who ask freedom from the regulation necessary for the common
good. Far too many middle-class American churchmen still
hold uncritically the Enlightenment faith in an automatic
providential harmony of egoisms whereby private vices become public virtues. The contribution of Protestant ethics to
the moral regulation of early capitalism has become an actual

impediment to its intellectual comprehension and moral regulation of late monopoly capitalism, while Roman Catholicism,
rooted in the moral conceptions of older aristocratic and present
classes can analyze the present crisis more objectively. American Protestants have been concentrated on the land and in the
upper classes in the cities and have had the least personal experience with the more bitter fruits of recent economic development. No one could have been expected to foresee the spiritual
and moral effects of the factory system, or of the sudden
urbanization of unprecedented proportions of the population.
No one foresaw, either, the international dynamics of economic
imperialism, and good Christian folk at home in Europe and
America had not the slightest comprehension of the vast and
well-grounded resentment being stored up against their civilization in distant lands and seas. On the contrary, the very fact
that unregulated capitalism was pursuing the line of least
resistance and revolutionizing colonial areas lulled Western
Christians for an unprecedented span of years at the turn of
the nineteenth century into a deluded sense of the remarkably
pacific nature of their new economic and political order. In-
credulity and incomprehension have been perhaps the dominant
mood of American Christians confronted by the world wars
with their clashing imperialisms, their series of social revolutions and the world-wide rise of color against the West.

The involuntary support from American Protestants for this
consolidation of a new industrial feudalism functions in a
variety of ways. The educated half of the clergy are socially and
culturally associated with the classes from which the elite of
economic life arise. The sophisticated approach to innocent
parsons at gracious social occasions or with well-edited bro-
chures, not to speak of the controlled press, can scarcely be
matched by the ill-bred protests of the oppressed, who, moreover, support very few churches. And the churches themselves

are involved in the whole structure of investment in the amount of some billions of dollars, an investment managed conservatively, but still according to current business ethics, which from any inclusive point of view are antisocial to a dangerous degree. The great majority of respectable heads of families in the churches, clerical and lay, are also directly accessory to the process. We are all in a sense held captives in this province and made to serve as hostages and witnesses of respectability by those who prefer to work behind the scenes. Every man who takes out an insurance policy has delivered his resources for shaping the economic life of the country into the hands of strangers. He does not know whose social policy he is voting for, whether Sewell Avery's or those of the garment industry. Well might he feel the discomfort T. S. Eliot has stated:

> I am by no means sure that it is right for me to improve my income by investing in the shares of a company, making I know not what, operating perhaps thousands of miles away, and in the control of which I have no effective voice—but which is recommended as a good investment. I am still less sure of the morality of my being a money-lender: that is, of investing in bonds and debentures. I know that it is wrong for me to speculate: but where the line is to be drawn between speculation and what is called legitimate investment is by no means clear. I seem to be a petty usurer in a world manipulated largely by big usurers.[1]

Can it be said that American Protestantism even recognizes the vice of usury?

Among the more pathetic situations is that of the Christian who has become aware of the moral ambiguity of the governing

---

[1] *Idea of a Christian Society* (London: Faber & Faber, Ltd., 1939), p. 103.

policy of the captains of industry and the barons of finance, the danger of the "servile state" as well as of the leadership of labor unions, and determines to hold himself neutral, or, on invitation, to arbitrate now and then. Probably a majority of seminarians aspire to this role, and probably many of them will occupy it, thus demonstrating the establishment of the American Protestant church. The manipulators of corporate wealth, who have a near monopoly on the press, the radio, and two or three less cautious clergymen, need only to point to the dignified and merciful abstention of these pillars of society to administer a rebuke to all disturbers of the social sanctities. Every clergyman who does not make himself felt to the contrary is so much more dead weight in the chariots of the rulers of this world. The withheld vote of the neutral is in effect a vote for the stronger and implies the judgment that the stronger is also the more righteous. And for every such implied judgment clergy and laymen shall one day answer. Let us hope their condemnation will not be the condemnation of the whole Church!

2. THE LOST PROVINCES: PERSONAL RELATIONSHIPS

When we turn from the ethical issues involved in the non-personal relationships of Christians to those where personal give and take is a constant factor, the variety of types and problems becomes unmanageable. No longer are there clearly defined organizations such as states or cartels, but a vast inter-locking network of groups and associations, social, cultural, educational, recreational, each presenting its peculiar moral opportunities and temptations. With no claim whatever of exhaustive analysis, consequently, we shall restrict our dis-

cussion to two types of social relationships of particular importance, racial adjustments, and the family, and conclude with
some observations on the changing character of ecclesiastical
institutions.

Race

An unfortunate aspect of our recent recognition of the forgotten ethical factors of impersonal group relationships has
been a certain distraction from a Christian concern for other
individuals. To be sure, we are more conscious of the self-
aggrandizement in paternalistic charity, but we take refuge
in organized social welfare, a kind of Western equivalent to
Tibetan prayer wheels in the assumption that mechanical
efficiency can improve on personal concern. We would re-
arrange men sociologically to suit our own aesthetic or rational
preferences. How little we think of straining our family conveniences to take in the homeless and hungry! There are too
many of them. We sincerely wish they could all be well-fed,
well-washed, pleasantly sociable bourgeoisie like ourselves, but
we will not and cannot face the immeasurable suffering of the
world and its claim on us and our routines. We habitually walk
by on the other side ninety-nine times out of one hundred. The
love that so loved the world does not burn evidently in us.
We are too ready to substitute resolutions or institutions for a
personal engagement, a "concern" in the Quaker sense. Yet the
Gospels make clear that the signs of the presence of the Reign
among us are to be most readily detected in our relations with
other individuals.

Arnold Toynbee has done us the service of identifying caste
as the peculiar spiritual deformity we share with India. Atheist
Russia is more obedient than Christian America or Britain to
the God of Jesus Christ on this momentous issue. In that broad

belt of Moslem countries from the Atlas Mountains to the Himalayas, black, white and brown live on terms of complete equality. Racism in Japan and China is almost entirely the deadly imitation of our own. The Roman Catholic peoples of the Mediterranean are largely free of it, so that American Army officials found it necessary in the first World War to warn the French not to "spoil" Negro troops, even by giving them due credit, since Negroes are considered inferior persons in the United States. It was, of all the world's statesmen, House, Cecil and Smuts, the representatives of Protestant cultures, who blocked the general declaration of racial equality at the Paris Peace Conference. Of all the nations of the world those who share with Nazi Germany the distinction of having written race into their statute law, the British Dominions, Dutch colonists and the United States stand alone, all predominantly Protestant, all so-called "democracies." And during the second World War the presence of American troops with their Nordic arrogance in societies such as Latin America where races and colors have lived together for generations was often justly regarded as an invasion as morally sinister as outright Nazi propaganda. In too many quarters of the world, American troops were ambassadors of evil and ill-will. Decent people everywhere fear our contagion.

Perhaps the most impressive Christian witness of all has been made by those Christians of other races who have borne the arrogance of the white without bitterness. Dean Thurman once compared the sufferings of the Apostle Paul at the hands of mobs and Roman police with those of an American Negro. When Paul was beaten he had only to say, "I am a Roman citizen," to receive apologies. But an Arkansas Negro lying in a ditch and beaten by a gang of Baptists cannot efficaciously protest, "I am an American citizen," or, "I am a Christian, too."

He will be beaten until his tormentors tire. And the depth of loyalty, charity and forgiveness of American Negro Christians is something before which we can all stand only in shame. The Christian Japanese, also, with reckless chivalry displayed their courteous devotion to American missionaries at the beginning of the last war at the very time when in the name of racism all American citizens of Japanese descent on the Pacific coast were brutally abused. As we American Protestants stand before our brethren in Christ of other races who despite all hold fellowship with us, would we could say in literal truth of that power of Christ to forgiveness which lies in them, "Surely he hath borne our sorrows and carried our griefs; he was wounded for our transgressions and bruised for our iniquities and by his stripes we are healed." Yet the God of righteousness is not mocked forever, and for those who cannot cleanse themselves, rough cleansing is often provided.

The family

The one great province of social relations which the Church still occupies and defends with conviction is that of the family. In the ancient world and in many sections of the non-Christian world today the good news of Christianity has meant a revolution in the position of woman and in respect for children. On these questions nearly all Christians still expect and welcome ethical guidance from the Church.

Yet the organic and cultural functions of the family also have been profoundly corroded by the rationalization of our industrial society. Despite all ecclesiastical manifestoes about a living family wage, Christian employers are unable to pay such a wage generally and most working-class families are prematurely broken by economic necessity. Mother and children work and the home becomes simply a common dormitory and restaurant. Middle-class families suffer only in less degree, especially in urban centers. The psychological tensions vary with the cultural situation from the patriarchal Jewish family and the erotic preoccupations of Vienna, which gave Freud his chief categories, to the inhibited and hard-driven husbands, the lonely and aggressive wives and the undisciplined children of the American middle-class family. Nearly everywhere the cultural and educational and religious functions of the family have disintegrated. Families no longer entertain themselves with music, sketching, writing, handicraft such as trained the early years of the great artists and writers of Western cultures. The movies and the radio are today the chief family recreations. They involve neither creative activity nor group interaction and the children grow up culturally inarticulate. Family religion is in like straits. The Reformation made every hearth an altar and family devotions were the universal education of children in the relation of worship to the common life and the trivial round of daily duties. Today it is rare to find in a city even a minister's family with regular religious worship. Protestantism can only return to Roman Catholic practice and restore daily worship in the churches.

Even with regard to sexual morality itself, the Church seems on the defensive. In the popular mind the position of the churches here is "puritanical," and this impression is partly justified. Such a "puritanical" code likely enough produces less personal and social suffering and conflict than the cult of the flesh which the popular mind, with perhaps equal accuracy, associates with the main body of psychiatric theory and praxis. Authoritarian puritanism will not hold the youth of industrial society, however, and the Church desperately needs a rational sex ethic and discipline. Clergy as well as laity are confused here, and because of their injudicious counsel on such matters the clergy are in danger of losing their functions to rivals perhaps even less competent but more plausible. This confusion is perceptible also in seminaries, where an all too large group of students involve themselves in unhealthy complications and burdens of guilt, to their damage and that of the Church. Yet we must recognize the essential solidity of the Christian family ethic, even under these ominous and increasing pressures. This solidity is of no small significance for society.

The political, economic, social, cultural and educational institutions and movements of our civilization, divorced as they largely are from moral and religious direction, are still redeemed in great measure by the religiously trained personnel which is constantly poured into them from Christian families generation after generation. It is difficult to assemble the evidence on these matters, but the conclusion is highly probable that Christian families produce a disproportionately large group of the socially useful members of the community, including many that have no further relation with the churches themselves, and, on the other hand, a still more disproportionately small share in the criminals, social parasites, broken homes of the nation. The clearest instances here are the children of the parsonage, who, as every sociologist knows, achieve distinction in all sorts of walks of life far more frequently than any comparable group. A sense of duty and personal integrity, a respect for objective fact, an acceptance of responsibility within the community, emotional balance and a serviceable intellect seem to be frequent by-products of Christian homes even when more specifically religious insights are not transmitted. Through its steady cultivation of the Christian home the Church determines far more of the ethical direction of modern society than a superficial observer would guess. The Church is vaguely felt on all hands to be a guide and support to the family, and many men

and women who before the birth of their children never had
occasion to seek religious or ethical communities of any sort
turn up in churches as their families grow. With only the haziest
notions of what Christianity means they will look there for
something they sense is good for their children and their life
together.

3. DISINTEGRATION IN CHURCH LIFE

Having surveyed the several provinces of social relationships,
from those still acknowledging a Christian duty to those out of
control of any conscience, those of impersonal and public character, and some of private and personal character, we may now
profitably return to the organized center of Christian activity
and study what changes have been made in the institutions of
the churches themselves by the disintegration of Christian discipline.

Loss of community

We find first of all that with the loss of ethical discipline
the churches have ceased to represent real communities. This
loss is often obscured by the striking display of conviviality
and homeyness in some churches, which is a symptom of the
substitution of class and cultural affinities for Christian conceptions and purposes. This is the community of the service
club, of the social and business stratum, not of the Church.
Many small-town parishes are still genuine community parishes,
where families attend as groups, with shopkeepers and their
clerks, farmers and hired men, bankers and doctors and
teachers, rich and poor, old and young. And while the farmers
no longer own their land, and the merchants and bankers are
controlled by corporative decisions they do not understand, and

the ablest children and the profits of productions always seem somehow to end up in the big city, nevertheless there is in such a parish a mutuality of daily association and a network of personal moral relations which seek and find clarification and reconciliation and blessing from the Father of all.

But consider the usual city parish! Who are these people who come to worship of a Sunday? How many of them are neighbors and desire to bring the frictions and joys of neighbors to a common judgment? How representative is the delegation from the several levels of industry and commerce? Why, we are lucky if we have the whole family. For these people come from all over the city, and most of them live nearer another church than they do to this one. This congregation is not a community, it is probably the personal following of this particular preacher. Jones likes him, but Mrs. Jones does not, so she goes to the Episcopal church with John, who belongs to the scout troop there, and Mary goes to the Baptists because they have the liveliest coke parties for the young people. It is remarkable indeed that the preacher is able to make the service significant at all to the audience, for we can scarcely say "congregation."

We think of the Church as a realm apart from daily living. Shorn of its larger ethical responsibilities the Church has relinquished its discipline and become merely an association for worship and for ministry to individuals among those who commit their chief moral decisions and ultimate loyalties to the organizations of political and economic power. The newspapers have sections titled, "the World of the Churches," and when one passes through the looking glass into this mysterious realm, one breathes a spiritual atmosphere heavy with cant. On all sides one may observe clergymen and practitioners of "professional religion" oiling, fitting and repairing the apparatus of churchmanship. Reluctant laymen are cornered and captured and domesticated as Sunday-school teachers, boy-scout leaders, financial campaign managers and dutiful Sunday listeners. Here and there sits a mystic manicuring his soul. And if you look too markedly interested, one of the harried clergy will step out of his treadmill for a moment to catch you by the collar and ask, "Brother (or Sister), how can I make my preaching and worship really significant to my people?" Nobody really believes all this makes any difference on the other side of the looking glass.

What difference *does* it make? Genuine worship is the celebration of realities discovered in common endeavor. But we have so little common endeavor to celebrate or redirect! The impressions, desires and standards of the politics, business and amusements about us dominate great stretches of our conscious life. In all this there is little or no awareness of God or obedience, but rather the pursuit of success, sensuality, national egoism. Most of the time we are sharp-eyed, skeptical modern men and women, concentrated absolutely on very relative goals and standards. The kingdom of God has been largely replaced as the organizing focus of our lives in our workaday decisions and dreams by the quasi-Moslem heaven whose description is never a day out of our sight and hearing on radio, movie screen, car cards, billboards, store windows. If we are to count in also the hours, sleeping and waking, when our subconscious and unconsidered volitions are indistinguishable from those of the men and women who never pass beyond the looking glass for esoteric Sunday concerns, then we may well wonder what difference it does make. If we were to lose our religion, how would anyone ever know it on weekdays? "Religion" has become a hobby, like the cultivation of folk dancing.

Irrelevant idealism

On any Sunday morning ten thousand pulpits quiver with the vehemence of orators declaiming about the "ideals" of Jesus, and seeking to raise America by mere enthusiasm to new heights of family or business integrity or optimism about international organization. Since this is the prevailing American idiom, we must use it at least as an apologetic device. Yet much preaching of "ideals" has the same effect as the reading of *True Confessions* and *Modern Romance* by girls of humdrum lives. It is a kind of daydreaming, a pursuit of irresponsible fancy into realms where knighthood is still in flower, and it can be indulged in until it is preferred to any realizations with actual and ornery people. Such schizophrenia is a fair description of great groups of American Protestant churchmen who have actually settled down into the perverted enjoyment of daydreaming in the pulpit about world peace or economic justice, but who will find forty reasons for not discussing restrictive covenants in the parish, or the antiunion drive which several of the trustees are pushing, or the larger implications of the tariff lobby from the local industries. These concrete issues seem so complicated and relatively petty, whereas an active man can steer some new resolution of universal scope through two or three church assemblies and the Federal Council, and make his mark in the world of the churches as a coming man, a bit radical perhaps, but a really broad-gauge fellow. In consequence of such "ethical" crusades the churches of America have several times outlawed war and the atomic bomb, industrial strife and the exploitation of other races—in India.

The ministry

This spiritual embarrassment of American Protestantism focuses on the vocation of the ministry. We have the curious situation of a primarily prophetic tradition become socially established and converted into a primarily priestly one. The best American ministers, for all the talk about prophetic preaching, are overwhelmingly priests, nursing the needs of their individual parishioners with faithful care, but trimming their public declarations and the action of their congregations rather carefully to what the traffic will bear. There are various ways of trimming. One of the most popular is scapegoating, with the liquor trade preferred. Commercialized alcohol involves serious issues, but there are deeper reasons why church groups so frequently make rum the primal curse of modern civilization and pursue it as if here they could staple down the spiked tail of Lucifer himself. This is the common device of the journeyman preacher. The aristocrats of the trade have subtler techniques. There is, for instance, the tacit conspiracy by which the more discerning clergy and their congregations ease their consciences, the preachers by telling a good bit of truth in the pulpit, and the congregation by submitting to listen, both thereby preparing to return more comfortably to their fraternizing with evil. Radical decisions can thus be rendered unnecessary by radical talk.

There must be preachers of the word, and yet a certain moral ambiguity always attends the profession. How shall they preach redemption who give so little evidence of being redeemed, or ultimate truth and holiness who are so rarely ultimately truthful or holy? We preachers spend our lives telling of how other men sacrificed theirs. In fact we make a living out of it. There is an account of two escaped prisoners from a prison camp in China, who made their way to the threshold of safety after arduous travel and desperate hazards. They had been associated for years in the nationalist movement in China, the one a worker, the other a publicist. But in sight of freedom the worker stopped. "You go on," he said, "and with your brilliant gifts tell the world what we are fighting for. I am going back so that when you write you can dip your pen in my blood and the world will know that we mean what we say." There is the burden of proof that always lies on the clergyman, to convince the world that he means what he says.

There is no doubt but that the American Protestant clergy as a group have a far more adequate conception of the implications of the Gospel for the whole community than have the laity, and have produced a series of prophets of some stature. That clergy, nevertheless, bear a major share of the responsibility for the hesitancy of American Protestantism to recognize its minority status and bear an incisive witness. The clergy are afraid of lay leadership, of youthful initiative, of able women. The local parson insists on being *the* bellwether of his flock and is jealous of his sovereignty within the scope permitted him by his trustees. The clergy as a whole specialize in devices for keeping up the appearance of successful congregational life without the reality. Within the limits of local propriety they are interested in anything to draw a crowd, but nothing which would give that crowd a specific practical intention, and thus offend some folk, unless it be some well-thrashed scapegoat like strong drink. Say nothing offensive, say nothing peculiar, say nothing down to earth, say nothing locally applicable, say nothing, but say it effectively. Similarly, as we observe how the elder statesmen of the denominations execute their trust in trivial matters, we are sometimes relieved to know that the larger responsibilities of Christian ethics no longer lie in their hands. Yet there is some reason to think that the relationship works both ways and that the reason small men are permitted to exercise authority is because the authority is so limited that more capable men are not interested. If the Christian community were to begin to form a common mind on an ethical issue of major importance it would, one suspects, discover a leadership commensurate with the task.

For there is little doubt that much, if not most, of the ethical endeavor of Protestant Christians is expended in religiously anonymous or neutral organizations. This practice began in the Evangelical Revival at the end of the eighteenth century, when hundreds and thousands of convinced Christians spilled out into all sorts of reform and humanitarian committees and societies: temperance societies, peace, antislavery, prison reform, societies for the education of women, of adults, of the poor, co-operatives, the labor movement, all sorts of charities and institutions. This ethical fertility of the Protestantism of the last century and a half and its individualistic and unchurched character are among the most striking aspects of this pietist "Methodist" epoch of our history. And still today the best lay leadership of Protestantism is found here, active in an indefinite variety of enterprises for the common good and in great measure doing so out of gratitude to the mercies brought to them in Christ and in the desire to submit themselves and society to his Lordship. The obligations they have assumed and the opportunities they still feel before them are often the chief obstacles before the pastor who would enlist their services in more strictly ecclesiastical functions. Here is the great hidden reservoir of Protestant ethical virility and lay leadership, a reservoir slowly ebbing in un-co-ordinated and wasteful expenditure. For with the passage of time and the severance from their religious sources, these various agencies and institutions become established and secularized, and the Christian leadership is increasingly assimilated to a pragmatic secular humanitarianism, the American "common faith." The emergent problems of our culture, meanwhile, are problems concerning the very structure of

society and are to be answered no longer by individual philan-
thropies independently of the Christian fellowship.

Just as we have still this hidden reservoir of Christian ethical
virility, we must still reckon also with the latent religious fellowship of the Church which bursts to the surface surprisingly
under tension to achieve its ancient function of reconciliation.
The savage disruption of fellowship brought by national wars
only illustrates the unconquered life of the hidden Church.
Thousands of Christian soldiers did one another to death in the
last war, acknowledging one common Lord and faith and
baptism and one common hope of God's reign. And have not
some at least told us that precisely in the most merciless
struggle, in some momentary pause, there hàs broken upon
them a moment of illumination in which they saw how a merciful Judge could accept and purify their ambiguous efforts
and by the total travail of his Church effect some new thing
beyond the partial vision of any? Again, pacifists and soldiers
have confessed a similar experience to each other. Christians
on either side of this decision have often felt keenly that their
own witness has been a partial if necessary one, that it has been
clouded with much evil and empty of much good which
should have been served. They have come to realize that those
who would do Christ's work in our world can often scarcely do
so singly, but only as special organs of one great body. Into
the sense of moral failure and guilt has come the assurance of
justification if not sanctification by the Lord of history. Even
our atomized parishes today are not wholly deprived of such
fleeting insights in the conflicts of daily labor, and in our common worship still it is not rare for congregations to draw into
focus all these fragmentary insights and abortive overtures and
to realize before God the actual fact of their common brother-

hood in sin and forgiveness, despite the institutional and habitual denial of that fact in society.

4. THE RENAISSANCE OF CHRISTIAN SOCIAL RESPONSIBILITY

Among the churches generally the last fifty years, at least, have been marked by a most impressive recovery of the Christian moral conscience. This recovery, moreover, largely antedates the encroachments of totalitarian states into the spiritual and moral life of the modern peoples. Within Protestantism this is a recovery of responsibilities felt before the pietist and individualistic era. The recovery was a futile gesture in Imperial Lutheran Germany and scarcely perceptible at all in Orthodox Russia, or in Roman Catholic Spain and Latin America, but in England, France, the United States, Belgium, Switzerland and Catholic Germany, a new tide was evidently coming in. The most conspicuous institutional affirmation of this new concern falls to the credit of Leo XIII, and the most familiar symptoms to Americans are the "social gospel" from Josiah Strong to Walter Rauschenbusch, with its outcome in the denominational social action committee and in the Federal Council of Churches. On the whole the movement has been strongest in the Protestantism of the Reformed tradition, particularly in Britain and America, and in Roman Catholic minorities in Protestant cultures. There are exceptions, however, as with the Anglo-Catholics, who have supplied far more than their share of intellectual leadership, both theological and sociological, as well as devoted and intelligent parochial practice. The Life and Work Movement, now of the World Council of Churches, has unified and stimulated this growing conception of the necessity for Christian political and economic and social ethics, especially in the great conferences at Stockholm and Oxford. In America the diffused impact of this movement on general political and social thought has been notable, going far to effect the transition from the nineteenth-century individualistic utilitarianism last championed in authority by Mr. Hoover, to a more solidaristic conception of society and the social welfare state. It still remains to be seen, however, whether this revival will reach the mass of laity, or whether it will signify only a deepening of the clerical vocation, somewhat like the Oxford movement of a century ago.

Indeed, the revival has come to a temporary standstill as the churches have discovered how long and how difficult is the road back to Christian moral autonomy and what mighty secular or pagan movements, sometimes with the disposal of political power, bar the path. American Protestantism, also, is permeated with cultural nationalism, and resists the decisions necessary to give it an incisive and unique witness to that culture. What is needed is such a clearing of the air, and the recognition of Christianity as a frankly minority movement. Then Christians would have to learn to live in two cultures, as have the Jews for centuries: first, the ethic and practice of the Christian life within a forming Christian community, and, secondly, the co-operation in common citizenship with "men of good will"— Marxists, secular humanitarians, devotees of "the democratic way of life," nationalists of the milder species, or whomever, on some minimum basis of "natural ethics." The difficulty will not be on this latter level, at least for the institutional churches. They will keep their institutional continuity and their adaptability to American culture to the very threshold of outright and deliberate hostility to religion. The difficulty will be to define a role within Protestantism for the growing cells of the new autonomous Christian communities.

The hesitation of the churches to proceed with the program already tentatively blocked out for a recovery of independence and Christian moral discipline is in the last analysis a well-advised fear of inviting persecution. The consensus of Christian political and economic discussion tends unmistakably to a declaration of war on capitalism and on the sovereign national state, neither of which organizations lacks means or willingness to defend itself. In fact, the question will be whether the churches would even be permitted to define a program of action at all. The channels of communication are already largely monopolized in America by secular powers. The public schools increasingly undertake to teach a whole philosophy and way of life, and increasingly pre-empt the time and energies of children. The Church can no longer reach more than a fraction of American children, and these for no more than an odd hour or two. The next generation as a whole is growing up with no religious heritage whatever. A secular philosophy again is overwhelmingly dominant in the newspapers, radio programs, movies which reach young and old alike. Ecclesiastical institutions may survive as they make themselves channels for the presentation of the more idealistic aspects of this secular cultural nationalism, but the very survival of Christianity *within* the churches has become problematical. Christianity, even in America, faces today as never before in Western history, the serious danger of cultural strangulation.

The ethic and practice of the Christian life within a forming Christian community, nevertheless, is the passionate desire of those abler and more earnest folk who yearly fall away from the churches in silent despair. It is the demand of many of our best veterans who caught a glimpse under great stress of what the Church should and might be. It is the hope of the leaders of the Student Christian Movement in the colleges and universities. The best and most promising of our people would like to be faithful Christians in their political and economic and social relations, but they are balked not merely by an increasingly secular society, but also by a pervasively unfaithful Church. There could be no more complete mockery of this hunger for Christian ethic than to invite these searching folk to engage in the young people's program or the couples' clubs or the men's societies of nine hundred and ninety-nine out of one thousand American churches. No wonder they go socialist or cynical! The Christian ethic cannot be achieved by individuals; it requires a community. And how can Christians win their way to such community when across the roadway lies the vast, inert, bloated hippopotamus of American Protestantism?

Community and discipline

And how miraculous is the result of any actual congregational decision to ethical self-discipline! Two superannuated elders withdraw and one millionaire trustee, and forty active men who haven't been in church for ten years appear on Sunday to see what is going on. The newspapers catch at it, all the other nearby churches fuss and flutter and it is talked about in Rio de Janeiro and Bombay. A church stood for something important! In Chicago a Presbyterian congregation elected to support the rights of a Negro family who had moved into a white district and were being threatened with fire and assault. The whole congregation escorted the family home and in the street before the residence worshiped while the neighbors listened in wonder. Since that day that church has known a strange experience: the Bible, and with it the Body of Christ, has come alive. There is a new sense of the meaning of a revelation of God in the events of history. Or again in Europe on the eve of this war, very similar decisions were made on the subject of anti-Semitism in Holland, France and elsewhere. Similar results followed: the Word of God was recovered and heard once again. And out from one limited decision of Christian morality there radiated a whole new vista of Christian discipline. Many are the Christian youth, again, who felt themselves impelled to take a pacifist stand in the recent war as the only possible expression for them of a Christian loyalty. Once taken, that simple action quickly revealed its limitations, but also its implications. If they really meant their Christian moral witness, they discovered, there was a wide range of other disciplines to be accepted and lived out. But they had begun somewhere!

Such decisions must often be one-sided. Such mistakes are far better than the mistake of the churches of Laodicea and Protestant America. It will be years and perhaps a revolution or a military defeat before the whole Church in America comes to one incisive mind on any broad range of the ethical challenges propounded by our secular society. Even one, such as racism, would vastly clear the air. But in the meantime there must be a crystallizing of voluntarily disciplined groups *within* the churches, men and women banding together as in the old Methodist class meetings or early Friends meetings, to think through and live out a new voluntary Christian discipline in racial relations, in industrial conflict, in sexual and family ethics, in regard to living standards, investments and numerous other issues. Out of such efforts and the repercussions they create among the parishes, a common mind may crystallize with some rapidity. Much of this burden must be carried by the laity— physicians, teachers, social workers, carpenters, teamsters, students, housewives—because they are better informed and more numerous and often more religious than the clergy.

In such self-disciplined groups many of the ethical proposals now made by Christian groups for the nation at large would find their proper role and lose their moral ambiguity. If Christian pacifists would recognize the difference between their personal obligations as Christians, and the political alternatives which a national and non-Christian state faces today, they might win more respect for Christian pacifism and less distrust as an irresponsible and mischievous political lobby. If Baptists wish to eschew strong drink and Roman Catholics contraceptives, let them use the proper means of corporate self-discipline and not maneuver their views through legislatures representing folk who do not accept the same first principles. A Christian fellowship which maintains such self-control out of firm inner conviction wins more interest and support for its views than are to be had by governmental impositions.

But while some such recovery of a Christian community discipline and morality now lies heavy on our consciences, we should not romanticize the possibilities. Every Christianization of civilization must be a compromise and a formalizing of the Christian life. Such a minimum is necessary as an alternative to a common life like our present one, which senses no tension, no obligation out of which a compromise might be shaped. The Church must be emancipated from this civilization to which it has become assimilated. Yet as Protestants we can never forget that the autonomy of the institutional church is no good thing in itself, and that every ethical system sanctioned by such an independent institution in protest against secularism must itself always be tainted. If we take seriously any of our ideals or standards, of peace, personal purity, economic justice, racial fellowship, they quickly force us to the realization of our continued rebelliousness and profound guilt, of our driving motive of resentment, of our Pharisaism. The more devotedly we pursue our community obedience, the more certainly we will nourish our egoism. And while it is our duty to break our pride to these curbs in every aspect of our common life, we should do so in full realization that this will not be our fulfillment, and prepare to solicit unwearyingly the mercy of God who alone can give the peace and purity we cannot earn.

The Christian ethic, then, is not limited to the prudential calculation of consequences, like the dominant American utilitarianism, nor is it careless of all consequences in fine stoic pride. Our task is to find only our humble assignment and to fulfill that with all our strength, confessing continually our endeavor to pervert it to *our* achievement, and trusting ever in God for the issue. For we may act by trust in unseen powers and possibilities of creation and redemption on which a "realist" would not dare to venture, but which the saints have proved reliable if costly. The good news of Christianity is of power, power manifest and promising greater activity to come, of a power which has created a new community and requires men to labor and to pray in that hidden Church. We shall not be saved by that labor, neither we, nor our people, nor the world. Yet we must ever strive to serve the Lord in community, and we will be saved, if at all, by His grace.

FURTHER READING

DAWSON, CHRISTOPHER H. *Religion and the Modern State.* London: Sheed & Ward, Inc., 1935.

NIEBUHR, RICHARD. *Social Sources of Denominationalism.* New York: Henry Holt and Company, Inc., 1929.

NIEBUHR, REINHOLD, PAUCK, WILHELM and MILLER, FRANCIS P. *The Church Against the World.* Chicago: Willett, Clark & Company, 1935.

TROELTSCH, E. *Social Teachings of the Christian Churches.* New York: The Macmillan Company, 1931.

SUBJECTS AND MEMBERSHIP OF THE COMMISSIONS

COMMISSION I-A

VOLUME I. *The Challenge of Our Culture*

CLARENCE T. CRAIG: *Chairman*
JAMES LUTHER ADAMS
ELMER J. F. ARNDT
JOHN K. BENTON
CONRAD BERGENDOFF
BUELL G. GALLAGHER
H. C. GOERNER
GEORGIA HARKNESS
JOSEPH HAROUTUNIAN

WALTER M. HORTON
JAMES H. NICHOLS
VICTOR OBENHAUS
WILHELM PAUCK
ROLLAND W. SCHLOERB
EDMUND D. SOPER
ERNEST F. TITTLE
AMOS N. WILDER
DANIEL D. WILLIAMS

COMMISSION I-B

VOLUME II. *The Church and Organized Movements*

The Pacific Coast Theological Group:

RANDOLPH C. MILLER: *Chairman*
JAMES C. BAKER
EUGENE BLAKE
KARL MORGAN BLOCK
JOHN WICK BOWMAN
ELLIOTT VAN N. DILLER

GALEN FISHER
ROBERT M. FITCH
BUELL G. GALLAGHER
CYRIL GLOYN
GEORGE HEDLEY

203

JOHN KRUMM
PIERSON PARKER
MORGAN ODELL
CLARENCE REIDENBACH
JOHN SKOGLUND
DWIGHT SMITH
FREDERIC SPIEGELBERG

EVERETT THOMSON
ELTON TRUEBLOOD
AARON UNGERSMA
HUGH VERNON WHITE
LYNN T. WHITE
GEORGE WILLIAMS

Guests of the Theological Group:

JOHN H. BALLARD
THEODORE H. GREENE
EDWARD OHRENSTEIN
EDWARD LAMBE PARSONS

HOWARD THURMAN
STACY WARBURTON
FREDERICK WEST

COMMISSION II

VOLUME III. *The Gospel, The Church and The World*

KENNETH SCOTT LATOURETTE: *Chairman*

EARL BALLOU
JOHN C. BENNETT
NELS F. S. FERRÉ
JOSEPH FLETCHER
HERBERT GEZORK
EDWARD R. HARDY, JR.
ELMER HOMRIGHAUSEN
STANLEY HOPPER
JOHN KNOX
BENJAMIN MAYS

WILLIAM STUART NELSON
RICHARD NIEBUHR
JUSTIN NIXON
NORMAN PITTENGER
JAMES McD. RICHARDS
LUMAN J. SHAFER
PAUL SCHERER
WYATT A. SMART
GEORGE F. THOMAS
FRANK WILSON

COMMISSION III

VOLUME IV. *Toward World-Wide Christianity*

O. FREDERICK NOLDE: *Chairman*
EDWIN R. AUBREY

ROSWELL P. BARNES
JOHN C. BENNETT

ARLO A. BROWN

E. FAY CAMPBELL

J. W. DECKER

H. PAUL DOUGLASS

CHARLES IGLEHART

F. ERNEST JOHNSON

CHARLES T. LEBER

HENRY SMITH LEIPER

JOHN A. MACKAY

ELMORE N. MCKEE

LAWRENCE ROSE

STANLEY RYCROFT

MATTHEW SPINKA

A. L. WARNSHUIS

A. R. WENTZ

ALEXANDER C. ZABRISKIE

VOLUME V. *What Must the Church Do?*

HENRY P. VAN DUSEN